FOR THE GLORY OF GOD

Fulfilling the Christian Purpose in the Messiness of Life

Chris Watts

For the Glory of God Copyright © 2021 Chris Watts.
All Rights Reserved Worldwide.

Cover picture by Karl Magnuson at unsplash.com.

Visit www.wattsintheword.com for articles, podcasts, and more!

Scripture quotations are (unless otherwise noted) from the ESV® Bible (The Holy Bible, English Standard Version®), copyright © 2001 by Crossway, a publishing ministry of Good News Publishers. Used by permission. All rights reserved.

ISBN-13: 9798613616275

Dedication

While ultimately the honor of this book goes to God, it is fitting to pay "honor to whom honor is owed" (Romans 13:7). This book would not have happened without the influence of three people.

First, my father Douglass Watts, who inspired in me the pursuit of knowledge. He is the person I turn to when I want to make sure my thoughts and conclusions are consistent and in order, and a person I am very proud to call "dad."

Second, my wife Tracy, who keeps me going when I want to give up. She is my first and last editor, and the person who makes sure compassion is not lost in the logic.

Finally, my late father-in-law Stan Mitchell, who encouraged me to pursue my writing. He saw in me a talent I wasn't sure I possessed. Without his influence, I would never have seriously considered writing a book. I don't know if he can read this where he is, but I hope so.

Table of Contents

1. The Christian's Purpose? 1

2. The Language of Glory 10

3. False Glory:
Things that Make it Impossible to Glorify God 16

4. Glory by Yourself:
The Battle in the Heart and Mind 29

5: Glory with the Church:
How Division Diminishes God's Glory 40

6: Glory in the World, Part 1:
Being "In" but Not "Of" 52

7. Glory in the World, Part 2:
The Importance of Holy Identity 65

8. Glory through Sex:
Confronting the World with God's Glory 76

9. National Glory:
When We Glorify the Wrong Thing 98

10. Digital Glory:
A New World 117

11. Financial Glory:
The Power and Danger of Choice 131

12. Broken Glory:
Glorifying God when it Hurts 146

13. Glory in Freedom:
When our Purpose is Confusing 157

1. The Christian's Purpose?

There are three most important questions, questions that people of all cultures and civilizations have wondered about, the ones that matter the most to the most people. These aren't questions of survival but of *meaning*. They aren't necessarily the deepest or the most obscure or the most philosophical, but they are the most *significant* – the ones that have the most riding on the answers.

1. Where did we come from?
2. Why are we here?
3. Where are we going?

Of course, these aren't the only questions that matter. But these form the core of human religious, philosophical, and scientific endeavors. From the origins of life and the universe to the question of what happens when we die, and the meaning of everything in between, we all want to know the answers to these questions. Fortunately for us, the Bible has answers!

WHERE DID WE COME FROM?

Then God said, "Let us make man in our image, after our likeness. And let them have dominion over the fish

> *of the sea and over the birds of the heavens and over the livestock and over all the earth and over every creeping thing that creeps on the earth." So God created man in his own image, in the image of God he created him; male and female he created them.*
> *- Genesis 1:26-27*

We do not have to wonder at our origins or the origins of the universe. We, like everything that exists, came from God. However, humans specifically were created in a very special way, in the "image of God."

Where Are We Going?

> *Then the King will say to those on his right, 'Come, you who are blessed by my Father, inherit the kingdom prepared for you from the foundation of the world…'*
> *Then he will say to those on his left, 'Depart from me, you cursed, into the eternal fire prepared for the devil and his angels.'*
> *- Matthew 25:34, 41*

Likewise, we do not have to wonder about our end. Whether or not the Lord returns before we die, we will all stand before judgment, to either be with the Father or be cast from His presence for all eternity. This is the sure destination of all of humanity.

Why Are We Here?

It's the middle question that is the most difficult. It's not that the Bible is silent on the matter; rather, the opposite is true. Most of Scripture deals with this exact question! The problem is that the question is too broad and nebulous. How many commands are there in the Bible? What about in just the New Testament? How many things are we told to do; how many examples are we given to follow? How can we possibly distill all the vast amount of instruction into a singular purpose, an overall aim for our lives?

Yet, when we do examine the totality of Scripture, we can indeed find a common thread, an overarching theme to all the commands, the examples, and the stories of Scripture. There *is* something we are supposed to do all the time:

> *So, whether you eat or drink, or whatever you do, do all to the glory of God.*
> - 1 Corinthians 10:31

This is the main text for our study together. It is an explicit command that is all-encompassing. "Whatever you do" does not leave anything out, does it? Would even something mundane like going to the grocery store fall under the umbrella of this command?

The implication is that it is possible to glorify God in all our actions. While this is an explicit command, there are more subtle passages on the topic. In speaking of the eventual kingdom to come, Isaiah proclaims these words of the Lord:

> *Fear not, for I am with you; I will bring your offspring from the east, and from the west I will gather you. I will say to the north, "give up", and to the south, "do not withhold; bring my sons from afar and my daughters from the end of the earth, everyone who is called by my name, whom I created for my glory, whom I formed and made."*
> - Isaiah 43:5-7

Why did God create those who would be called by His name? "For my glory," He says. He made us for His own exaltation! Even of those who are not called by His name Paul later says:

> *What if God, desiring to show his wrath and to make known his power, has endured with much patience vessels of wrath prepared for destruction, in order to make known the riches of his glory for vessels of mercy, which he has prepared beforehand for glory.*
> - Romans 9:22-23

If the "vessels of mercy" are those who would receive mercy, those who would be part of the group Isaiah says are sons and daughters of God, then who are the "vessels of wrath"? Wouldn't that be those to whom the Lord will say "depart from me, you cursed"? Why did God create these vessels of wrath? "In order to make known the riches of His glory"!

In either deliverance or destruction, God will be glorified. All creation exists to serve this singular purpose: to bring about the exaltation and glory of God! Yes, there are myriad aspects of life, but none can be wholly separated from this grand purpose. The choices we make add up in totality to God's glory, one way or another.

> *You are the light of the world. A city set on a hill cannot be hidden. Nor do people light a lamp and put it under a basket, but on a stand, and it gives light to all in the house. In the same way, let your light shine before others, so that they may see your good works and give glory to your Father who is in heaven.*
> - Matthew 5:14-16

> *Beloved, I urge you as sojourners and exiles to abstain from the passions of the flesh, which wage war against your soul. Keep your conduct among the Gentiles honorable, so that when they speak against you as evildoers, they may see your good deeds and glorify God on the day of visitation.*
>
> - 1 Peter 2:11-12

Thus, we see the importance of our Christian example! The Christian is not only to glorify God directly by his or her actions, but to encourage other people to do so as well. Our lives should motivate even non-Christian people to give glory to God!

This singular purpose, the answer to the question "why are we here?", cannot be separated from the other two questions. *(1) Where did we come from*? We were created by God, very specifically for His glory! Even in the mere acknowledgment that God is the creator, we glorify Him by acknowledging His singular power and supreme authority. *(2) Where are we going*? We will either be "vessels of wrath" and thereby show the riches of His glory by contrast, or we will be "vessels of mercy" and exalt God in our salvation. In the admission that judgment is coming, we glorify God in our confession that He alone holds the authority to judge and the power to save or destroy.

There are many ways we serve as Christians and many specific activities we are commanded to do, but each is in service to a larger goal: to glorify the Creator, the Judge, our Lord and Father!

Now, don't misunderstand. There are many facets and particulars of Christian service and life. We should not and cannot discount things like evangelism or stewardship or parenting or any other specific manifestation of the new life in Christ. Rather, the point is this: in any act of service to the Lord, we glorify Him!

If there is one thing that might supplant our purpose of glory, it would be evangelism. The call to "make disciples" is one of the fundamental jobs of all Christians. We know that Jesus himself came "to seek and to save the lost" (Luke 19:10). We cannot truly feel good about our relationship with God if we are not trying to show others the light of His Word.

But there are things we are commanded to do that are not evangelistic, like worship, communion, or treating our parents well. Could these things serve some sort of missional purpose? Of course! The public assembly is a valuable point of contact with the lost, and we know that we, in a sense, "proclaim the Lord's death" (1 Corinthians 11:26) when we partake in the Lord's Supper. But these acts do not need to be evangelistic in order to be righteous. We can and should worship even when there are no lost people around. We can and should participate in the Lord's Supper even if there are no visitors in the assembly. But if these things are not glorifying to God, then they are in vain! If our worship did not exalt God, was it even worship? If our communion did not elevate the sacrifice of Christ, did we even know what we were doing? Thus, we see that while some aspects of our Christian walk don't necessarily evangelize, all glorify!

What Does it Mean to Glorify?

What does it mean to glorify God or to give glory to God? Perhaps John the Baptist said it best:

> *Now a discussion arose between some of John's disciples and a Jew over purification. And they came to John and said to him, "Rabbi, he who was with you across the Jordan, to whom you bore witness—look, he is baptizing, and all are going to him." John answered,*

The Christian's Purpose

> *"A person cannot receive even one thing unless it is given him from heaven. You yourselves bear me witness, that I said, 'I am not the Christ, but I have been sent before him.' The one who has the bride is the bridegroom. The friend of the bridegroom, who stands and hears him, rejoices greatly at the bridegroom's voice. Therefore this joy of mine is now complete. He must increase, but I must decrease."*
>
> *- John 3:25-30*

From a cosmic perspective, John was a particularly important person. He was prophesied about in the Old Testament and praised by the Lord himself! Yet, when confronted with Jesus's growing popularity and his own waning fame, John's impulse was to glorify God; *to make Jesus increase while he decreased.*

What exactly was increasing and decreasing? In this case, it was fame and esteem, concretely measured by the number of followers Jesus and John had. More people were following Jesus, and less people were following John. The idea of God increasing while we decrease is the core of what glorifying Him is all about! In John's mind it was good for more people to follow Jesus! This is the heart of glorifying; that God will in some way increase.

What would be the opposite of glorifying or elevating God?

> *...you then who teach others, do you not teach yourself? While you preach against stealing, do you steal? You who say that one must not commit adultery, do you commit adultery? You who abhor idols, do you rob temples? You who boast in the law dishonor God by breaking the law. For, as it is written, "The name of God is blasphemed among the Gentiles because of you."*
>
> *- Romans 2:21-24*

Our actions could, instead of elevating God and making Him look good, make Him decrease in the eyes of the lost. People might see our behavior and think "well, I want nothing to do with their God!" How terrible this is, for our actions to decrease God's glory rather than increase it! We want God to be elevated in the eyes of the lost because of our actions and teachings! We want Him to increase, either in the amount of praise He receives or the number of followers He has or in the implied exaltation of our humble submission to His will. We definitely don't want our actions to result in Him receiving any less of these things!

So when God says that He created us "for His glory," this is what He means. In our existence, in everything we do, God should be praised, elevated, honored, and made to look good. His honor and praise must increase, rather than decrease, both among His children and in the eyes of the world.

The Rest of This Book

But, as we said, this is too broad. There are a thousand ways to glorify God. If it were simple, the Bible wouldn't need to be so long. The Bible writers spend much ink outlining how to glorify God in myriad circumstances. That is what the rest of this book will be about: how to glorify God, in whatever we do.

Specifically, how do we glorify God in some of the harder or more controversial aspects of our specific time and place? Sometimes, glorifying God is easy, or at least uncomplicated. We know we should praise Him, evangelize, and obey Him, but how do we glorify God in the messy, complicated parts of life? The topics we will address are important but might be hard to talk about. I ask that you approach this with an open mind and a humble heart. May this study bring glory to Him!

Digging Deeper

1. The human search for *meaning* ebbs and flows over the course of a lifetime. What life circumstances make people considerer deeper questions of purpose and meaning, and when do people ignore or forget such questions?

2. When in your life have you been the most concerned with a deeper search for meaning? What was going on at the time? What were some of the best ways people helped you?

3. It is not uncommon for people to say that evangelizing is the primary purpose of the Christian and the church. Why is this incorrect? Does that mean evangelism should not be one of our main goals? Why or why not?

4. Is it uncomfortable to think that eternal wrath and judgment can bring glory to God? How can we come to grips with this idea and present it to the world in a compassionate way?

2. The Language of Glory

It is all well and good to know that the primary purpose of the Christian life is to glorify God, but what exactly is glory? When God says that He created us "for His glory," what does that mean? What does God expect from His people when He commands us to "glorify" Him?

Glory in the Old Testament

There are two primary words that are often translated "glory" in the Old Testament (*kabod* and *tip'eret*). These words are fairly straightforward. *Kabod* basically means "glory" or "honor" and might be associated with wealth or status or some high office. The word is most often applied to God, to describe His position and status as Ruler and Creator of all things. It is sometimes used to describe His presence ("the glory of the Lord filled the temple" in Ezekiel 43:5).

It can also be used to denote the sense of reverence or respect that a person has toward those with great wealth, status, or position. Thus, to glorify God in this sense is to recognize His status, position, and awesome attributes, and to give Him the reverence those things deserve.

The second word *tip'eret* is also often translated "glory" but also "splendor." This word has less to do with status and more to do with appearance, or something appearing glorious. In Esther 1:4 King Artaxerxes displayed his *kabod* and *tip'eret* with a celebration lasting 180 days. The important thing was for people to see his glory and splendor. This is what glorified him (gave him glory). The word is sometimes translated "beauty" or "beautiful" (as in Ezekiel 16, describing the effect of fine jewelry).

Again, when applied to the Lord, this word describes His splendor, strength, and beauty. Thus, to glorify God in this sense is to recognize the splendor and value of the things He has done, to ascribe to Him the value He is worth, and to recognize His beauty.

GLORY IN THE NEW TESTAMENT

The Greek words most often translated "glory" are a bit different. As is the case with many Greek words, the primary word for "glory" (*doxa*) can be appropriately translated several different ways depending on context. Fundamentally, *doxa* is a word concerning appearance, seeming, or reputation. Satan, when he tempts Jesus in Matthew 4, shows Jesus "all the kingdoms of the world and their glory" (4:8). Luke uses the word in Luke 14:10 to describe the honor or glory associated with sitting in the best seat at a feast. Paul uses the word to describe the overwhelming "brightness" of the light that appeared to him on the road to Damascus (Acts 22:11). The word can be translated "splendor," "glory," "honor," or "praise" and is most often used to describe God and His aspects. God is inherently glorious.

Thus, as in the Old Testament, to glorify God in this sense begins with recognizing God's value, splendor, worth, and position. We glorify God because He *is* glorious. He is the most valuable, powerful, important, authoritative being in existence. Glory is the recognition and proclamation of this fact.

This leads us nicely to the second word used to denote glory in the New Testament, *kauchaomai*, which is a verb that most basically means "to boast." It can be negative (when improperly boasting about yourself) or positive (when properly boasting about God).

The concept of glorifying God through boasting is at the heart of 2 Corinthians 10-12. Paul was concerned that others had come to Corinth, claiming to be apostles and preaching a different gospel to the one Paul had preached there. They were disparaging Paul, calling him weak (10:9-10). Paul responded by boasting about all the earthly badges of honor that he might have used to elevate himself in their eyes (11:21-28). But the whole time he was boasting of his success and physical gains, he kept calling himself a fool (11:1, 16-18). Paul considered boasting about earthly things to be foolish! Note the common theme throughout these chapters:

> *But we will not boast beyond limits, but will boast only with regard to the area of influence God assigned to us, to reach even to you.*
> - 2 Corinthians 10:13

> *"Let the one who boasts, boast in the Lord." For it is not the one who commends himself who is approved, but the one whom the Lord commends.*
> - 2 Corinthians 10:17-18

> *If I must boast, I will boast of the things that show my weakness.*
> - 2 Corinthians 11:30

Finally, we come to the end of Paul's defense against these

so-called apostles:

> *So to keep me from becoming conceited because of the surpassing greatness of the revelations, a thorn was given me in the flesh, a messenger of Satan to harass me, to keep me from becoming conceited. Three times I pleaded with the Lord about this, that it should leave me. But he said to me, "My grace is sufficient for you, for my power is made perfect in weakness." Therefore I will boast all the more gladly of my weaknesses, so that the power of Christ may rest upon me. For the sake of Christ, then, I am content with weaknesses, insults, hardships, persecutions, and calamities. For when I am weak, then I am strong.*
> *- 2 Corinthians 12:7-10*

This is the same attitude that John the Baptist had, isn't it?

Paul understood that glorifying God meant talking about and boasting about the things that made God look good or elevated God in his life. It wasn't about the things Paul was good at or what Paul had accomplished; it was about how God had empowered Paul to do those things! To boast about himself was foolish. Glorifying God means boasting about Him, His power, and His activity in our lives!

THE BEGINNINGS OF GLORY

Glory is a matter of reputation, appearance, and status. It is a matter of value and worth. God is glorious because He is the Creator, the only true and living God. He is glorious because of His love and mercy and grace. He is glorious because of His sacrificial love and mighty power.

We can now draw some conclusions about what it means to glorify God. It begins by the conscious admittance and recognition of these Divine attributes. It begins with faith! Faith is the first act of glory. Our belief and faith in God is the first way we honor and acknowledge His value and status.

We must first believe that He is splendid before we can marvel in his splendor. We must first trust in His mercy before we can praise Him and thank Him for it. We must first submit to His authority before we can proclaim it in the world.

Throughout the rest of this book, we will use a lot of synonyms and terms: magnify, praise, glorify, exalt, elevate, and more. But these all have their foundation in this root idea: to glorify God is to believe in and recognize all the myriad aspects of his glory and to respond with these kinds of actions.

To put it another way, to glorify God is to demonstrate to Him that we see and know Him and understand that He is majestic and splendid. The second part of glorifying God, then, is showing others how awesome and glorious He is. Let's dig into how we do that!

Digging Deeper

1. List all the synonyms you can think of for "glory" or "glorify". How many of these words do you use on a regular basis? How often do you use these words in thinking about or talking about your Christian life?

2. What are some good ways to "boast" about God? How often do you boast about God in your conversations with other Christians? What about with the lost?

3. How does having faith glorify God? Why must faith be the first way that we glorify Him?

4. It's easy to turn glorifying God into a way to glorify self ("oh I'm so God-glorifying, look at me!"). How can we avoid this trap? What sorts of attitudes or phrases turn God-glorifying efforts into self-glorifying?

3. False Glory: Things that Make it Impossible to Glorify God

Before we can talk about how to give glory to God in "whatever we do," we need to talk about some attitudes and ideas that get in the way of glorifying God. These are thoughts, emotions, and habits that, despite all our good intentions, will prevent us from elevating God on a personal level and before the eyes of the world.

The first danger is this: if we aren't careful, we can easily start defining "glory" the way the world does. What we are trying to discover are the sorts of things that exalt, elevate, or glorify God. It is of utmost importance that we remember that we, as the created, do not get to dictate what glorifies the Creator. He gets to set the terms and say how He wants to be exalted. The things we do to honor humans might not be the things that God wants us to do to honor Him. On the other hand, things that we would never do to elevate another human might be glorifying in God's eyes. He has the prerogative to dictate what exalts Him, because He is the Creator!

What sorts of things get in the way of glorifying God the way He deserves and wants? How could we even know what He wants anyway?

Pride and Selfishness

Let's return to the story of John the Baptist. Remember what he said to the disciples that warned him about Jesus:

> *The one who has the bride is the bridegroom. The friend of the bridegroom, who stands and hears him, rejoices greatly at the bridegroom's voice. Therefore this joy of mine is now complete. He must increase, but I must decrease.*
> - John 3:29-30

This is a good attitude, the right attitude, but we could imagine a different response. He could have been angry that Jesus was stealing all his followers. He could have had the attitude that "I did all the work, so I should have the glory." This is the kind of mindset that comes from pride and selfishness.

When we care more about ourselves than about God, we will stop glorifying Him. This is true even if we keep going to church, singing out in worship, and helping the poor. It's not just about *what* we do but *why* we do it. We might be fooling others, but we aren't fooling God.

Jesus was very clear about actions that may seemingly elevate God while being based on selfish motives. Three times in Matthew 6:1-18 Jesus cautions against merely outward expressions of righteousness designed to deceive anyone looking on. He says do not give to the poor (6:2-4), pray (6:5-15), or fast (6:16-18) in order to be "seen by them" (6:1). God would rather you glorify Him in private than attempt to give Him false glory in public. Things that might elevate God publicly do not glorify Him if they are done with selfish, prideful motivation.

Even if we do continue to do the right things in a public

setting, the longer our hearts are bent on our own glory, the farther from God's glory we will stray. Eventually pride catches up with us, no matter how well we hide it for a time. Our true natures will always win out, and when we do eventually stop "glorifying God," the contrast between what we did and who we were all along will dishonor God all the more!

Let us consider a contrast of two kings.

Saul's Presumption and Arrogance

Saul ruled over Israel during a time when the Philistines were a bitter rival nation. The Israelites and Philistines hated each other! In 1 Samuel 13, we read a story of an impending fight. The Israelites won a skirmish, and then the Philistines gathered in force, scattering the Israelite forces to the hills to hide in caves.

Now, we have to read a bit between the lines in this story (seriously, read 1 Samuel 13). We are told that Saul "waited seven days, the time appointed by Samuel" (13:8). We can only infer what was supposed to happen at this meeting from what happens next, but it seems clear that Samuel was going to meet Saul to sacrifice to the Lord to seek His favor for the coming battle. But Samuel was late, and the troops with Saul "followed him trembling" (13:7).

It's easy to see that Saul was worried about losing control of his troops. The Philistines were numerous and part of Israel's forces were already scattered. They needed the morale boost of the sacrifice and the power of the Lord's favor, so Saul didn't wait. He went ahead and offered the sacrifice (13:8-9), even though he was a member of the tribe of Benjamin and thus not allowed to offer such sacrifices.

We can understand Saul's motivation. The soldiers were

weary and downtrodden. Saul just wanted to give them a victory. He knew that he was God's anointed king, so surely God would have given him favor anyway. Why wait for a legally appointed priest to perform the sacrifice, when the result was a foregone conclusion anyway? If he waited any longer, the Philistines might get away or find his people!

> *As soon as he had finished offering the burnt offering, behold, Samuel came. And Saul went out to meet him and greet him. Samuel said, "What have you done?" And Saul said, "When I saw that the people were scattering from me, and that you did not come within the days appointed, and that the Philistines had mustered at Michmash, I said, 'Now the Philistines will come down against me at Gilgal, and I have not sought the favor of the Lord.' So I forced myself, and offered the burnt offering." And Samuel said to Saul, "You have done foolishly. You have not kept the command of the Lord your God, with which he commanded you. For then the Lord would have established your kingdom over Israel forever. But now your kingdom shall not continue. The Lord has sought out a man after his own heart, and the Lord has commanded him to be prince over his people, because you have not kept what the Lord commanded you."*
> *- 1 Samuel 13:10-14*

Remember, as a Benjaminite, Saul was not authorized to offer such sacrifices to the Lord without a priest, who could only be from the tribe of Levi. He was impatient.

He presumed that God would need to work on a mortal timetable. Note the explicit reason he gave Samuel for going ahead without him: "the people were scattering from him." So what? Why would it matter if the people were there or not? If

God was going to be with Saul through the battle, it didn't matter where the people were. He could have gotten it done with the soldiers in the hills or some other force that God would bring. Saul didn't see a way to win the battle without the forces he had brought, and he assumed that if he did not offer the sacrifice in time they would leave.

This assumption led him to seek the favor of the Lord in a "foolish" way. We can only conclude that he presumed it wouldn't matter that he wasn't a priest. After all, he was a king!

When confronted about it, he was not contrite or humble. He gave excuses (blaming it on the fear of the people and Samuel's lateness) instead of owning up to his sin. The very thing he wanted to have, the favor of the Lord, was the very thing he squandered in his haste and vanity! What was his punishment? "But now your kingdom shall not continue," said Samuel, "the Lord has sought out a man after his own heart."

What did this mean, that God wanted a man "after his own heart"? We will consider this in the next section, but Saul proved he didn't have the right heart by refusing to learn from his mistake. Just a few chapters later (1 Samuel 15), we read about the same attitudes. Commanded by the Lord to utterly destroy all of the Amalekites, Saul was victorious in battle, but instead of annihilating them as he was told to do, he did something else:

> *And Saul defeated the Amalekites from Havilah as far as Shur, which is east of Egypt. And he took Agag the king of the Amalekites alive and devoted to destruction all the people with the edge of the sword. But Saul and the people spared Agag and the best of the sheep and of the oxen and of the fattened calves and the lambs, and all that was good, and would not utterly*

destroy them. All that was despised and worthless they devoted to destruction.

- *1 Samuel 15:7-9*

At this point in the story we can only speculate about his motivations, but, again, he thought his own ideas were better than God's. He kept the best of the animals, either out of greed (wanting to keep them for himself) or arrogance (thinking he knew better than God what should be done with these things). However, God had commanded a specific thing and He was not pleased with Saul's presumption:

> *And Samuel said, "What then is this bleating of the sheep in my ears and the lowing of the oxen that I hear?" Saul said, "They have brought them from the Amalekites, for the people spared the best of the sheep and of the oxen to sacrifice to the Lord your God, and the rest we have devoted to destruction."*
>
> - *1 Samuel 15:14-15*

Again, note the shift of blame from himself to "the people." He was already hedging instead of owning up to his own decisions. Was it always his intention to sacrifice the animals to God? Did he begin the battle with that in mind or was he swayed later? We will never know, but for the purpose of the story it's irrelevant, because *that is not what God commanded.* Even if we assign to him the most gracious and best motivation possible, it would not have satisfied God. Saul does finally confess some amount of sin, but he still hedges, blaming the people for basically intimidating him into the sin (1 Samuel 15:24).

Twice Saul ignored God's explicit commands and did something he thought was better. Even if he really did have the best of intentions, it doesn't matter! God told him what He wanted, and Saul decided to do something else. No matter what his intentions were, he wasn't bringing glory to God, and we see that in God's reactions to him. Even though in both stories Israel ended up defeating the enemies of God, God was not pleased! And when Saul was confronted about his mistakes, rather than humbly admitting fault, he tried to shift the blame!

When we presume to know better than God, we stop glorifying Him, even if we have good intentions. When we aren't humble enough to admit our flaws and correct them, we will keep failing to glorify Him. What made Saul a man not "after God's own heart" was his unwillingness to wait, be patient, and bring victory to God's people *the way God expressly said He wanted it*. Presumption and arrogance were the things that kept him from being the kind of king worthy of the title! Only by reverently admitting that God does indeed know what He wants and knows what is best, will we humbly begin to seek actions and attitudes that glorify Him.

DAVID'S ACCEPTANCE AND HUMILITY

Fortunately, God had already found the man after His own heart. David wanted to bring glory to God so much. In the story of David and Goliath (1 Samuel 17), David was incredulous that God's people would bring shame on God by allowing their fear of the giant to control them. David knew that God was awesome and thought Israel was acting dishonorably by not trusting in Him.

Later, after David became king, he realized something that he thought was unjust. He worried that something was wrong in the kingdom of Israel, something that would ultimately detract from God's glory:

> *"See now, I dwell in a house of cedar, but the ark of God dwells in a tent."*
> - 2 Samuel 7:2

We understand David's impulse to glorify God, right? Why should David have this great house while God had a tent (the tabernacle)? David rightly assumed that God deserved whatever David could do to elevate Him. Maybe according to our human reasoning it would be a great honor for God to have David build him a proper building instead of a measly tent. Why should the Creator have a worse building than His anointed? Note God's response:

> *But that same night the word of the Lord came to Nathan, "Go and tell my servant David, 'Thus says the Lord: Would you build me a house to dwell in? I have not lived in a house since the day I brought up the people of Israel from Egypt to this day, but I have been moving about in a tent for my dwelling. In all places where I have moved with all the people of Israel, did I speak a word with any of the judges of Israel, whom I commanded to shepherd my people Israel, saying, "Why have you not built me a house of cedar?"'*
> - 2 Samuel 7:4-7

By the time of David's request, God had already established a theme in his dealing with the kings. If God had wanted a house of cedar, he would have asked David to build it! Later, when God wanted it, He commanded Solomon to build it. It wasn't as if a temple would have been dishonoring to God, but God wanted it on His own timetable. Fortunately, David was humble enough to seek the counsel of the Lord.

More than that, God turned it around on David and promised to elevate and exalt him (2 Samuel 7:10-16). So instead of David building a house to honor God, God was going to build something to His own glory far surpassing anything David could have done.

How did David respond? What did he do? Did he reject the word of the Lord and go ahead with his plan anyway?

> For you, O Lord of hosts, the God of Israel, have made this revelation to your servant, saying, "I will build you a house" Therefore your servant has found courage to pray this prayer to you. And now, O Lord God, you are God, and your words are true, and you have promised this good thing to your servant.
> - 2 Samuel 7:27-28

He accepted God's word and didn't try to push the issue. He realized that God has the right to dictate His own glory!

Well sure, you might say, *it's easy to accept God's will when it is beneficial for us, but what about when it is hard?* It is true that it is easier to accept God's desire for glory when the arrangement benefits us (as it was for David here). How did David respond to God's will when it wasn't in his favor?

Consider one of David's greatest failings, when he had an affair with Bathsheba and murdered Uriah by proxy (2 Samuel 11-12). Surely this did not glorify God! When he was confronted with this sin, how did David respond?

> David said to Nathan, "I have sinned against the Lord."
> - 2 Samuel 12:13

How is this confession different from Saul's? We see no excuses or shifting of blame. We see no hemming or hawing or delaying. As soon as the veil of his own hubris was removed and he was shown his sin clearly, David took full responsibility. He is more explicit in his confession in Psalm 51:

> *Deliver me from bloodguiltiness, O God,*
> *O God of my salvation,*
> *and my tongue will sing aloud of your righteousness.*
> *O Lord, open my lips,*
> *and my mouth will declare your praise.*
> *For you will not delight in sacrifice, or I would give it;*
> *you will not be pleased with a burnt offering.*
> *The sacrifices of God are a broken spirit;*
> *a broken and contrite heart, O God, you will not despise.*
> *- Psalms 51:14-17*

He understood what God wants: humility and contrition when we sin against Him! Even after this heinous sin, this is what enabled David to continue to bring glory to God. Notice what he said he will do: "my mouth will declare your praise."

This praise is all the more powerful because of God's punishment for the sin he had committed, which he was certainly informed about before he wrote Psalm 51:

> *And Nathan said to David, "The Lord also has put away your sin; you shall not die. Nevertheless, because by this deed you have utterly scorned the Lord, the child who is born to you shall die."*
> *- 2 Samuel 12:13-14*

Can you imagine how Saul would have reacted to such a discipline? Yet the first thing David does after the death of the child is worship (2 Samuel 12:20). If David had put his own will above God's, or thought that he had known better than God, this punishment surely would have driven him from the

Lord. Because he humbly accepted the will of the Father, he was able to glorify God even when his heart was broken and his life was shattered. We will return to this story in a later chapter, because it is such a good example of attitudes and behaviors that glorify God.

TRUE AND FALSE GLORY

If we want to glorify God, we must accept what He says and do it to the best of our abilities, instead of presuming that our ideas about God's glory are better than His own. If we want to glorify God, we need to humbly admit our failings and strive to do better, instead of hedging and shifting blame onto someone else. If we want to glorify God, we must exalt him in good times and in bad, even when it feels like we are being disciplined by Him. Arrogance and closed, proud hearts are the attitudes that will make it impossible to glorify Him, while humility and submission will lead to His glory!

Finally, consider the story of Nadab and Abihu, who offered "strange" or "unauthorized" fire to the Lord as an act of worship.

> *Now Nadab and Abihu, the sons of Aaron, each took his censer and put fire in it and laid incense on it and offered unauthorized fire before the Lord, which he had not commanded them. And fire came out from before the Lord and consumed them, and they died before the Lord. Then Moses said to Aaron, "This is what the Lord has said: 'Among those who are near me I will be sanctified, and before all the people I will be glorified.'" And Aaron held his peace.*
>
> *- Leviticus 10:1-3*

God's response to this strange offering is so enlightening.

What did God say to Aaron to justify killing his sons? "I will be sanctified…and glorified." To be sanctified means to be regarded as holy or set apart as something better or purer. As we have seen, to glorify means to recognize God's power and position and elevate and praise Him for it. No matter what their intentions were, their offering did not honor God nor were they considering Him as holy. God will not just accept whatever glory we decide to offer Him; He demands and deserves the specific kind of glory that He has already delineated!

We must regard God differently than we regard our parents or friends or bosses or even ourselves! He is to be viewed in a special way. The things you do to honor the important people in your life may or may not be the kind of thing that God will view as honoring. The minute we start thinking about God like we think about anything or anyone else, we will stray from glorifying Him.

How, then, can we know what God wants? How can we glorify Him the way He wants? Let's dive into some of the things we need to know if we want to glorify Him.

Digging Deeper

1. Has someone ever presumed something about you that wasn't true? How did it make you feel? How should that affect the way you seek to glorify God?

2. What are some common misconceptions people presume about God or the Bible today? Where do they get these false ideas about God and His word?

3. How can we be sure we aren't presuming things about God that would lead us to stop glorifying Him the way He wants? How do we avoid the failings of Saul, Nadab, and Abihu?

4. What are some of the key attributes or attitudes David possessed that led him to have such a heart for God? Do you possess these traits? If not, how can you cultivate these in your own heart and mind?

4. Glory by Yourself: The Battle in the Heart and Mind

What percentage of your life do you spend by yourself? Of course, this will vary wildly from person to person, based on things like children, spouses, jobs, personalities, etc. But even excluding sleep (which you may or may not do alone), you probably spend a significant portion of your day alone.

We know that Jesus took time to be alone, to pray and commune with the Father (Mark 6:45-47; Matthew 14:23). In Matthew 4, he spent 40 days by himself, preparing himself for the work to come! This is to say nothing of the incidental time he would have had by himself throughout the three years of his ministry. Therefore, we know it must be possible, and in fact important, to glorify God in solitude, without the distraction, influence, or pressure of social interaction. Fundamentally, a relationship with God is a personal one. No one can make you glorify God, and no one can remove you from that relationship except for you (Romans 8:31-39; Hebrews 6:4-8; 2 Peter 2:20-22). This doesn't mean we don't need others. It simply means that the glory we give to God starts in our private moments and thoughts. The sum of these moments in turn determine our true character.

It is easier, perhaps, to focus on the glory we give to God

before and with others. We evangelize and thus glorify God through our teaching. We worship as a church and thus glorify God with others in the assembly. These are, by definition, public things but we know that the public glory we give to God must start inside ourselves. Our words and actions (eventually) flow from our hearts and minds:

> *And he said, "Are you also still without understanding? Do you not see that whatever goes into the mouth passes into the stomach and is expelled? But what comes out of the mouth proceeds from the heart, and this defiles a person. For out of the heart come evil thoughts, murder, adultery, sexual immorality, theft, false witness, slander.*
> - Matthew 15:16-19

As we have previously seen, one of the worst forms of false glory is the attempt to exalt God in public while we refuse to exalt Him in private, in our hearts. This is the core of hypocrisy, something Jesus condemned again and again. He condemned it in the Sermon on the Mount (Matthew 6, discussing works done to be seen by others), and he condemned even the religious rulers in Israel for it (Matthew 23, when he pronounces woes on the scribes and Pharisees for being hypocrites).

We have all probably heard some variation of "your character is determined by what you do when no one is looking". There is a lot of truth in this idea. Peer pressure is typically seen as a negative thing, but it can also influence people to do righteous things they wouldn't otherwise do. The end result of this kind of peer pressure is *hypocrisy,* when we act one way by ourselves but a different way around others.

The desire to be seen a certain way by others is a powerful force in our hearts and minds. However, if we are to glorify

God in everything we do, we must first bend our hearts to Him when no one is looking, when we are our most basic selves, with as few external pressures as possible. Only by becoming consistent in our actions, both alone and with others, can we avoid this hypocrisy.

THE EASY AND OBVIOUS

How do we glorify God by ourselves? Of course, we know this means that we shouldn't do bad things, even when no one is looking.

> *Flee from sexual immorality. Every other sin a person commits is outside the body, but the sexually immoral person sins against his own body. Or do you not know that your body is a temple of the Holy Spirit within you, whom you have from God? You are not your own, for you were bought with a price. So glorify God in your body.*
> *- 1 Corinthians 6:18-20*

It's almost so obvious it shouldn't be said, but I will say it anyway. Sinful behavior doesn't glorify God, so a key component of exalting God is cutting out sin from our lives!

However, the inverse is also true: we know that we should be doing good things, even by ourselves. In a certain sense doing good things by yourself is potentially more glorifying to God than avoiding sin is. "And your Father who sees in secret will reward you" (Matthew 6:4, 6, 18). When we submit to God's will and act righteously when no one is looking, there is no possibility that we are simply doing it to perform for others. Who you are in private demonstrates your truest priorities!

Practically, most of the things we do with others that

glorify God are things that we could do by ourselves. We could sing praises, pray to God, and learn from His word without anyone else. In fact, if you do not currently do these things by yourself, you should! We can even do acts of service that benefit others without anyone else being involved. How many people do things silently, without fanfare, that we all end up benefiting from? These things certainly glorify God!

But fundamentally, these all stem from something deeper. We can easily be motivated to do glorifying things with and for others by social pressures and influences. But when it's just you and God, and the social forces have been removed, you must find motivation in yourself. The real battle for God's glory begins and ends in our hearts and minds, the deepest part of our very being.

BEING TRANSFORMED

Let's look at perhaps the most interesting passage on this subject, from Romans:

> *I appeal to you therefore, brothers, by the mercies of God, to present your bodies as a living sacrifice, holy and acceptable to God, <u>which is your spiritual worship</u>. Do not be conformed to this world, but be transformed by the renewal of your mind, that by testing you may discern what is the will of God, what is good and acceptable and perfect.*
> *- Romans 12:1-2, emphasis added.*

The underlined part here is the controversial part. When we list various major translations of the passage, one after the other, we can see the difficulty that even experts have in translating this passage:

"...your spiritual worship." ESV, HCSB, NRSV
"...your reasonable service." KJV, NKJV
"...your reasonable service of worship." MEV
"...your spiritual service of worship." NASB
"...your true and proper worship." NIV

Remember the actual point of the verse: Paul wants you to "present your bodies as a living sacrifice." Of course, we know that we use our bodies at work, around the dinner table, or really in whatever we do. We use our bodies even when we aren't specifically worshipping God. The debated word here, translated either *service* or *worship*, or both (the MEV and NASB really copped out here, huh?), is *latreia*, which is indeed sometimes used in contexts that imply worship. But even when used in contexts that aren't talking specifically about worship, *latreia* is always used in ways that imply some sort of religious service or sacred duty. The word itself has more to do with the things we do for God than the specific act of worshipping God (See "service" in John 16:2, "duties" in Hebrews 9:6, and "worship" in Hebrews 9:1). Worshipping is one thing we do for our God, but it is not the only thing.

What is a sacrifice? In this passage and others, Paul connects and compares the sacrifices of the animals in the Old Testament, the sacrifice of Christ on the cross, and the life Christians live for God. We make that sacrifice when we put to death the old self and start living for God. Paul had already elucidated this process in Romans 6:

> *What shall we say then? Are we to continue in sin that grace may abound? By no means! How can we who died to sin still live in it? Do you not know that all of us who have been baptized into Christ Jesus were baptized into his death? We were buried therefore with him by baptism into death, in order that, just as Christ*

was raised from the dead by the glory of the Father, we too might walk in newness of life.

For if we have been united with him in a death like his, we shall certainly be united with him in a resurrection like his. We know that our old self was crucified with him in order that the body of sin might be brought to nothing, so that we would no longer be enslaved to sin.

- Romans 6:1-6

The sacrifice of Christ involved a death, and our sacrifice does too, even though we are still living. The crucifixion of the old self had a purpose, that "we might walk in newness of life."

How do we do this? That is what Paul is describing in Romans 12: we must be "transformed by the renewing of our mind." Repentance, confession, and baptism are the first acts of a mind that has started submitting to God, but it doesn't end there. When the old self dies, the old way of thinking must die with it. The transforming of our minds is a changing of the way we look at the world and the way we process it!

The question and answer given in 6:1-2 is then elaborated upon in chapter 12, where Paul uses the word "acceptable" twice. In order to glorify God, we must live in a way that is acceptable to Him (a life that is not lived in sin). Before we can do that, we need to know His will, or in other words, what things are acceptable to Him. God doesn't expect us to just bumble through and figure it out as we go. Vast swaths of both the Old and New Testaments contain specific, detailed information about how God wants to be glorified! The first step to glorifying Him is to start prioritizing His will and then learning what that will is. This is what it means to be "transformed by the renewing of our mind."

Consider again Nadab and Abihu and Saul. It's not that

they didn't know what God wanted. God had specifically told them! The reason their actions were rejected by God was that they knew what God wanted but instead chose to do something else.

This is a central theme in the way Paul talks about glorifying God. Over the course of Colossians 3:1-10, he told them they needed to "seek the things that are above" (3:1) and "set your minds on things that are above" (3:2). He listed a bunch of earthly qualities that would inhibit their ability to live for God (3:5-9). Then he told them:

> *Do not lie to one another, seeing that you have put off the old self with its practices and have put on the new self, which is being renewed in knowledge after the image of its creator.*
>
> *- Colossians 3:9-10*

What was the thing that was going to renew them, give them the "new self"? It was knowledge! The quest to glorify God begins in our hearts and minds. We kill that part of our heart that prioritizes self, and then we fill our minds with things that please God.

The things we think about are the things we do (most of the time). This is why advertising works; the commercial plants in your mind the product, and then you start thinking about it. The next time you are at the store you buy it instead of the competitor's product, because the company successfully implanted their product into your mind! What we think and what we care about comes out in the way we speak and act. Our priorities, obsessions, and focus all begin with thoughts.

> *For those who live according to the flesh set their minds on the things of the flesh, but those who live according to the Spirit set their minds on the things of*

> *the Spirit. For to set the mind on the flesh is death, but to set the mind on the Spirit is life and peace. For the mind that is set on the flesh is hostile to God, for it does not submit to God's law; indeed, it cannot. Those who are in the flesh cannot please God.*
>
> - Romans 8:5-8

That last line is so powerful: "those who are in the flesh cannot please God." If we can't please Him, can we glorify Him? When our minds are hostile to God, do we think we will be able to elevate or exalt Him?

This concept is at the very core of belief and repentance, isn't it? To repent is to change or turn your mind, leading to a new way of living. This change is the natural follow-up to belief. Once we put our faith in God and accept His word as true, then our very first response should be to try to mold our thoughts about the world into something in accord with that truth. From this process flows the changes in our actions!

Our thoughts are not just a means to an end or the thing that will help us eventually do glorifying things. Our thoughts themselves can be glorifying or dishonoring to God:

> *You have heard that it was said, "You shall not commit adultery." But I say to you that everyone who looks at a woman with lustful intent has already committed adultery with her in his heart. If your right eye causes you to sin, tear it out and throw it away. For it is better that you lose one of your members than that your whole body be thrown into hell.*
>
> - Matthew 5:27-29

Thoughts are not just the things that lead to sinful or righteous actions; *thoughts themselves* can be sinful or righteous. When we consider what it means to glorify God "in whatever you do," that must begin with the basic building blocks of our personalities and character. Your thoughts and feelings, more than anything else, are the truest expression of yourself, because it is from your thoughts that everything else flows.

The pursuit of God's glory begins with knowledge of, faith in, and discernment of His will. We become pure and blameless through *approving* what is excellent (Romans 12:2, Philippians 1:9-11). The word used in both places (*dokimazo*) carries the idea of "testing" or "scrutinizing." We must test and scrutinize our thoughts and beliefs, to see if they line up with the standard of God's will.

We can only do this through the transformation of ourselves, the changing of our will and the acquiring of knowledge. This enables us to love "more and more" and ultimately results in "the glory and praise of God" (Philippians 1:9-11). As opposed to what? What would be the opposite of this?

> *Brothers, join in imitating me, and keep your eyes on those who walk according to the example you have in us. For many, of whom I have often told you and now tell you even with tears, walk as enemies of the cross of Christ. Their end is destruction, their god is their belly, and they glory in their shame, with minds set on earthly things.*
> *- Philippians 3:17-19*

That last line is such a warning: "they glory in their shame." What shame? Paul is referring to the earthly things they have set their minds on and what those things have led them to do! These were the shameful things! When he says that "their god is their belly," he is talking about a person set on satisfying the body alone and forsaking eternal things. The result is clear: these are the "enemies of the cross of Christ"! Is that what we want to be?

SO WHAT DO WE DO?

It's hard to control our hearts and minds, the deepest parts of ourselves. It takes the most effort, because there's almost zero perceived accountability; no one knows and most people may never know. What do we think about? How do we feel about things? What do we let our minds linger on? From this flows our priorities, dreams, hopes, and plans. If we want to glorify God by ourselves, what should we do?

> *Finally, brothers, whatever is true, whatever is honorable, whatever is just, whatever is pure, whatever is lovely, whatever is commendable, if there is any excellence, if there is anything worthy of praise, think about these things. What you have learned and received and heard and seen in me—practice these things, and the God of peace will be with you.*
>
> *- Philippians 4:8-9*

If you want to glorify God spend more time reading and thinking about His Word and learning what He expects. No time spent in the Word will be wasted, and it will transform you into something truly glorious!

Digging Deeper

1. How often do you intentionally think about glorifying God when you are by yourself? Why is it so much easier to think about glorifying God when we are around other people?

2. Do you ever worship God by yourself or with your family? List some ways you could work worship into your individual and family schedules.

3. How different are your current thought patterns than they were around the time of your conversion to Christ? List some of the changes. If you are having trouble coming up with some, why could that be?

4. How can we recognize when we are failing to glorify God with our hearts and minds? What are some ways you could add accountability to this part of your life?

5: Glory with the Church: How Division Diminishes God's Glory

When we think about elevating, exalting, or glorifying God, a good subject to study is the temple construction by Solomon. It was constructed, over a long period of time and at great expense, specifically to give God glory:

> *And Solomon sent word to Hiram, "You know that David my father could not build a house for the name of the Lord his God because of the warfare with which his enemies surrounded him, until the Lord put them under the soles of his feet. But now the Lord my God has given me rest on every side. There is neither adversary nor misfortune. And so I intend to build a house for the name of the Lord my God…"*
>
> *- 1 Kings 5:2-5*

We previously looked at the passages detailing David's desire to build the temple and God's response. Solomon was allowed to do what David could not and "build a house for the name of the Lord my God." 1 Kings 5-9 goes into great detail about its makeup and construction: the best materials, the finest woods, the most valuable components. It was awesome and excellent, a building fit for the Most High. Truly it was a monument to God's greatness, and we know that God approved:

> *And when the priests came out of the Holy Place, a cloud filled the house of the Lord, so that the priests could not stand to minister because of the cloud, for the glory of the Lord filled the house of the Lord.*
>
> *- 1 Kings 8:10-11*

"The glory of the Lord filled the house of the Lord." How fitting! After the seven years of construction and the dedication of the holy place, God filled it with His very presence. The structure was grand, to be sure, but it was not *glorious* until God had entered it.

Once He had done so, the glory of that place was so great that the priests couldn't even bear to be in it! The temple would serve as the focus of God's public glory for centuries to come. But, even as this great place was finished, God reminded Solomon of something even more important:

> *Now the word of the Lord came to Solomon, "Concerning this house that you are building, if you will walk in my statutes and obey my rules and keep all my commandments and walk in them, then I will establish my word with you, which I spoke to David your father. And I will dwell among the children of Israel and will not forsake my people Israel."*
>
> *- 1 Kings 6:11-13*

While God's presence was in the temple in a very real way, God also wanted to dwell "among the children of Israel." Being with His people was more important than the great temple constructed for His glory. What would exalt and elevate God was not just the grand building but also the willing obedience of His children!

Destroying the Temple

God kept the temple language long after He stopped dwelling within the earthly structure. Paul, when talking to the church in Corinth, says:

> *Do you not know that you are God's temple and that God's Spirit dwells in you? If anyone destroys God's temple, God will destroy him. For God's temple is holy, and you are that temple.*
> - 1 Corinthians 3:16-17

The "you" in this passage is plural, though English doesn't really do that well. We might use the southern "y'all." We, collectively the *people* of God, are now the *temple* of God, the place where God lives on earth. Paul is very explicit about this ("God's Spirit dwells in you")! Just as the temple of Solomon was a monument devoted to God's glory, so should the church be! Yet, there is a warning in this passage not to "destroy God's temple." What destruction was Paul worried about? We know how we might destroy a building; indeed, Solomon's temple was destroyed and no longer exists! How would you destroy a collection of people?

This admonition to the Corinthians comes as the conclusion to a long discussion about unity and division in the church in the first three chapters of 1 Corinthians. If you want to destroy a building, you need to break apart the bricks, the joints, and the fasteners in order to separate each individual building block from the others and thus reduce the structure to nothing. If you want to destroy the temple of God's Church, you need to do the same, by destroying the connections between the various parts of the building (the individual people in the group).

This is what was happening in Corinth. In the first three chapters of the letter, Paul laid out for them how they were in danger of destroying God's temple, and the worst part was that they were doing it to themselves!

> *For it has been reported to me by Chloe's people that there is quarreling among you, my brothers. What I mean is that each one of you says, "I follow Paul," or "I follow Apollos," or "I follow Cephas," or "I follow Christ." Is Christ divided? Was Paul crucified for you? Or were you baptized in the name of Paul?*
> *- 1 Corinthians 1:11-13*

By dividing themselves by who preached to them or who baptized them, they were dividing the church. The end result was that what should have been a glorious, spiritual temple of God was reduced to being a regular collection of individuals:

> *For while there is jealousy and strife among you, are you not of the flesh and behaving only in a human way? For when one says, "I follow Paul," and another, "I follow Apollos," are you not being merely human?*
> *- 1 Corinthians 3:3-4*

Because of their division, they were no longer the spiritual building blocks of God's temple but were reduced to their basest, most mundane components (the flesh). Just a few verses later, he reminds them that they are the temple of God, as an appeal for them to put aside their faulty, divisive thoughts.

They were diminishing the temple of God! God's temple is one of the primary avenues of God's glory, and by reducing that temple, we reduce God's glory. If we allow the temple of God to be divided through division, strife, and jealousy, then we are contributing to the diminishing of God's glory.

A Glorious House

The Hebrew writer speaks of these matters as well:

> *For Jesus has been counted worthy of more glory than Moses—as much more glory as the builder of a house has more honor than the house itself. (For every house is built by someone, but the builder of all things is God.) Now Moses was faithful in all God's house as a servant, to testify to the things that were to be spoken later, but Christ is faithful over God's house as a son. And we are his house if indeed we hold fast our confidence and our boasting in our hope.*
> - Hebrews 3:3-6

In comparing and contrasting Jesus and Moses, the writer calls Jesus the builder and Moses part of the house. This makes sense; if the people of God are the house of God, then Moses is simply part of it. He was faithful and a great servant, but Moses did not build the house. Jesus, as the one who formed the structure, is worthy of the most glory. The Hebrew writer is explicit: "We are his house"!

Consider: if we truly seek God's glory above all, won't we want His house to be as grand and as excellent as it can be? If we are being formed in God's house by the builder Jesus, shouldn't we want Jesus to have as much glory as possible?

Let me be clear; this doesn't refer to the church building or the physical structure in which you worship (though I'm sure it's very nice). Paul is very clear that "God does not live in temples made by man" (Acts 17:24). Even Solomon, who built a place that God physically inhabited for a time, recognized this truth (1 Kings 8:27-30). All the passages in the New Testament epistles that talk about the structure, building, temple, or house of God refer to the *people* of God, united in purpose to provide God with a dwelling place worthy of His presence. Don't confuse the house of God with a mundane physical building.

The connections between us are the nails, the bricks, the mortar. The love we have for one another is the stuff that forms us into something greater than who we could ever be on our own. Our unity of purpose and thought is what makes this structure great! When we are divided, we create a temple for God that is run-down, dilapidated, and leaking. We create something not glorious at all. Would you want to live in a broken, run down house? Why would God want to live in such a place?

It's Not Just About Us

Solomon's temple was the thing that pilgrims came to see. It was the face of the Israelite religion to the world. When the nations looked at Israel and saw the grand temple, it told them something about the God of the Israelites: His power, His glory, His might. Because Israel was a physical, earthly kingdom, God's glory was demonstrated in physical, earthly ways.

Even though God's kingdom has transitioned to something spiritual instead of physical, the church should serve the same God-glorifying function in the world:

> *A new commandment I give to you, that you love one another: just as I have loved you, you also are to love one another. By this all people will know that you*

are my disciples, if you have love for one another.
- John 13:34-35

The relationships we forge with one another through love are what the world should see! When the world views the church (again, the group of people, not the building), they should be blown away by the love we have for one another! This is one of the primary ways we become the "light of the world" (Matthew 5:14). When the lost in your community experience your congregation, they should be motivated to "give glory to your Father who is in heaven" (Matthew 5:16).

If the world sees a group of people who hate each other, who fight all the time, who can't seem to agree on anything, who are apathetic about one another, and who don't seem to even like each other that much (let alone love each other), *this will reflect poorly on God.* If the goal is to elevate God in all things, then unity through love is one of the most important ways we can do that! This was one of the things Jesus prayed most fervently for:

> *I do not ask for these only, but also for those who will believe in me through their word, that they may all be one, just as you, Father, are in me, and I in you, that they also may be in us, so that the world may believe that you have sent me. The glory that you have given me I have given to them, that they may be one even as we are one...*
> - John 17:20-22

Is Jesus' prayer for His house been answered in your congregation? What does the world see when it looks at the group of believers you belong to?

Does it see a group where generations (boomers, millennials, etc.) all look down on each other and fight with each other, as happens so often in the world?

Does it see a group of people that doesn't really like to spend time together, where it seems like everyone can't wait to get out of the assembly?

Does it see a group of people that can't resolve disputes peacefully and instead airs conflicts in public spaces, real or digital?

Does it see a group composed of individuals all seeking their own good at the expense of others?

This is how the world operates, and if that is what the lost see when they look at God's temple, they will not see God's glory!

No one wants to live in a broken, leaking, run-down house. So, if people come to your fellowship and see such a structure, why would they want to be a part of such a thing?

How Do We Do It?

Paul is not subtle about the means of accomplishing the goal of elevating God: we must be unified in our understanding of Scripture, and we must constantly put other people ahead of ourselves.

> *Only let your manner of life be worthy of the gospel of Christ, so that whether I come and see you or am absent, I may hear of you that you are standing firm in one spirit, with one mind striving side by side for the faith of the gospel...*
> *- Philippians 1:27*

> *So if there is any encouragement in Christ, any comfort from love, any participation in the Spirit, any affection and sympathy, complete my joy by being of*

the same mind, having the same love, being in full accord and of one mind. Do nothing from selfish ambition or conceit, but in humility count others more significant than yourselves.
- Philippians 2:1-3

This is a group effort! No one can or should be an alone Christian! When we reduce our Christian walk to an individual effort, we rob God of the glory of His temple and reduce our effectiveness dramatically. If you are trying to "do Christianity" by yourself you won't be a part of a God-glorifying temple. How can I be clearer about this? If you think you can be a Christian without being a part of a congregation, you are not glorifying God. You are not contributing to the glory of God's temple, and you are thereby violating God's clear instructions about fellowship and unity!

If you are a member of a local congregation, what do you think of the people you worship with? Do you consider them at all? Do you think about them or pray for them at all?

It's easy to focus on the negatives. While it is true that in any group of people there will be some amount of conflict, that doesn't have to overshadow our purpose. Do we let conflict overwhelm our love for each other? Do we only think about the bad things people do and never look for the positives? Do we make a conscious effort to encourage one another even when we are mistreated, or are we always moaning about how we want to be the one who is encouraged? Encouragement is a two-way street! The temple of God needs all the parts working together, meaning that you will encourage and be encouraged in turn.

Ultimately, how we relate to and deal with each other is one of the primary factors in our continual attempts to glorify God:

> *We who are strong have an obligation to bear with the failings of the weak, and not to please ourselves. Let each of us please his neighbor for his good, to build him up. For Christ did not please himself, but as it is written, "The reproaches of those who reproached you fell on me." For whatever was written in former days was written for our instruction, that through endurance and through the encouragement of the Scriptures we might have hope. May the God of endurance and encouragement grant you to live in such harmony with one another, in accord with Christ Jesus, that together you may with one voice glorify the God and Father of our Lord Jesus Christ. Therefore welcome one another as Christ has welcomed you, for the glory of God.*
> *- Romans 15:1-7*

When we glorify God together, God's glory is exponentially increased. Jesus welcomed us into the house of God "for the glory of God"! When we bear with each other's failings and help one another, we exalt or elevate our savior and Creator. Just like the beauty of a song is greater when you add the complementary parts and harmonizing voices, so too is the beauty of God's house when all the various parts are fit together properly.

This begins with understanding our relationship with Jesus. We were all lost, weak, and hopeless, but Jesus welcomed us. So, when your brother or sister seems lost, weak, or hopeless, consider the structure that you are building together. When a house has a flaw or is damaged, do you just stare at it and hope it goes away? Do you just get angry at it? Of course not! You fix it and try to make it whole again. How can we who comprise this holy house make it more glorious for God who dwells in us?

> *Above all, keep loving one another earnestly, since love covers a multitude of sins. Show hospitality to one another without grumbling. As each has received a gift, use it to serve one another, as good stewards of God's varied grace: whoever speaks, as one who speaks oracles of God; whoever serves, as one who serves by the strength that God supplies—in order that in everything God may be glorified through Jesus Christ. To him belong glory and dominion forever and ever. Amen.*
>
> - 1 Peter 4:8-11

What kind of behavior leads to God's glory? When we love one another earnestly and show hospitality without grumbling, God is glorified! When we "serve one another" and use our varied gifts of God's grace, God is glorified!

Stop tearing each other down! Stop fighting and posting all your grievances for all the world to see. Stop bringing out every mistake, while ignoring the good your fellow Christians do. Stop complaining about how things are not exactly the way you want. It isn't all about you, and God deserves better!

When we allow strife and personal disputes to divide us, we diminish God's glory in the world. Brothers and sisters, I pray that we will never be found to be the cause of dimming God's glory by wrecking the house that He lives in. Truly "to Him belong glory and dominion forever and ever. Amen."

Digging Deeper

1. This week, make an intentional effort to use the word "church" only to describe the group of people, and not the building where you assemble. Use "church building" or just "building" every time you talk about the structure. After, consider if it was easy or hard, and why it was so.

2. There are always going to be differences between members of God's church. What can you do to prevent these differences from becoming conflicts and divisions?

3. List some things you are willing to give up in the name of unity and God's glory. List something things you are not willing to give up or compromise on. What made you put these items on each list?

4. How often do you bad-mouth or complain about "the church" or other Christians, especially in the company of non-Christians? How do you respond when you hear other Christians doing that?

6: Glory in the World, Part 1: Being "In" but not "Of"

I remember my mother telling me that as Christians, we must not just avoid doing evil, but also avoid "the appearance of evil, as the Bible says." She said this, or variations of it, often. Her point was (and is) that it isn't enough to be technically righteous; we also need to avoid situations that might be misunderstood or misconstrued as evil, regardless of whether or not they are actually sinful. This usually came up in the context of a girl I wanted to hang out with and why she was so insistent that we have a chaperone or be in public. "Mom!" I would protest, "you know I'm not going to do anything!" (and truly, I had no ill-intent). But she would always reply with, "even if you don't do anything wrong, people will assume you did. We need to avoid even the appearance of evil." Later, after I moved out, I tried to find the verse that tells us to avoid even the appearance of evil. This phrase does exist, but only in the King James translation of 1 Thessalonians:

> *Quench not the Spirit. Despise not prophesyings. Prove all things; hold fast that which is good. Abstain from all appearance of evil.*
>
> *- 1 Thessalonians 5:19-22 (KJV)*

Most of the other major translations have "every form of evil" at the end of verse 22, rather than the word "appearance". The word *form* has a slightly different connotation, but the word "appearance" is a fine translation. The same Greek word is used several other times in that sense (Luke 9:29, John 5:37) and is translated as "sight" in 2 Corinthians 5:7 (ESV).

But, even if "appearance" isn't what Paul specifically intended in 1 Thessalonians 4, there are other verses that convey the idea that righteousness is not just about our behavior or actions. It's about how our behavior and actions are perceived as well!

> *Beloved, I urge you as sojourners and exiles to abstain from the passions of the flesh, which wage war against your soul. Keep your conduct among the Gentiles honorable, so that when they speak against you as evildoers, they may see your good deeds and glorify God on the day of visitation.*
> *- 1 Peter 2:11-12*

We've looked at this passage already, because it uses one of the key phrases for our study: "that they...may glorify God." What is it that would cause those outside the kingdom to glorify God? They would only do this if we keep our conduct among them honorable! (We will come back to this idea of "honorable conduct" in a moment.) The next few verses continue the same thought, despite the fact that most modern Bibles put in a heading break:

> *Be subject for the Lord's sake to every human institution, whether it be to the emperor as supreme, or to governors as sent by him to punish those who do evil and to praise those who do good. For this is the will of*

God, that by doing good you should put to silence the ignorance of foolish people. Live as people who are free, not using your freedom as a cover-up for evil, but living as servants of God. Honor everyone. Love the brotherhood. Fear God. Honor the emperor.
- 1 Peter 2:13-17

We should, by the way we live, be able to "silence the ignorance of foolish people." In what way are they ignorant? If they are lost, they are ignorant of what is righteous, what things are good, and which actions are wicked. While everyone has some sense of morality in their conscience, those who do not know God or study His word do not have a complete understanding of God's standard of morality, and so they fill in the gaps of their conscience with their own standard. Thus, their ignorance would lead them to speak badly of us, unless we live lives of such purity that even those who are ignorant of God's standard have no means of accusing us.

What is the point? There are many actions or behaviors that may not be sinful but that we should still avoid simply because of how they will be perceived! We must consider how our actions will be perceived by fellow Christians, of course, but we should be just as concerned (if not more so) about how the lost will interpret our actions. The lost only have us to show them what God is like and what holiness is! We must concern ourselves with not just the doctrinally explicit righteousness of our behavior, but also how it might appear to others. We must consider how our actions could be twisted or misunderstood by those who are ignorant!

What is Honorable?

Let's return to that phrase in 1 Peter 2:12: "keep your conduct among the Gentiles honorable." Honorable is not just a matter of righteousness, but of perception! Paul expounds upon this idea in 1 Corinthians:

> *"All things are lawful," but not all things are helpful. "All things are lawful," but not all things build up. Let no one seek his own good, but the good of his neighbor. Eat whatever is sold in the meat market without raising any question on the ground of conscience. For "the earth is the Lord's, and the fullness thereof." If one of the unbelievers invites you to dinner and you are disposed to go, eat whatever is set before you without raising any question on the ground of conscience. But if someone says to you, "This has been offered in sacrifice," then do not eat it, for the sake of the one who informed you, and for the sake of conscience— I do not mean your conscience, but his. For why should my liberty be determined by someone else's conscience? If I partake with thankfulness, why am I denounced because of that for which I give thanks?*
> - 1 Corinthians 10:23-30

Paul knew and explained in Romans 14:14-20 and 1 Corinthians 8:4-6 that the meat sacrificed to idols held no inherent rightness or wrongness: the morality of the meat was and is a matter of perception (and conscience). Here in 1 Corinthians 10 we find more support for my mother's position (don't tell her I said that): *All things are lawful, but not all things are helpful.* How often do we consider how our actions will be perceived and understood by the lost, as opposed to simply considering the Biblical rightness or wrongness of them? Too often we consider whether something is lawful or permitted, without considering whether it is helpful or beneficial. Righteousness is not just about the explicit letter of the law; it's about the way our actions affect and might be perceived by others. Our ability to influence the lost might be harder to gauge than the explicit commands and instructions of the Bible, but it is just as important.

Now, by this point you may be wondering what this has to do with glorifying God. Remember, our actions are what will lead the lost to either glorify or dishonor God. Our central verse of this study is literally the next verse in 1 Corinthians 10:

> *So, whether you eat or drink, or whatever you do, do all to the glory of God. Give no offense to Jews or to Greeks or to the church of God, just as I try to please everyone in everything I do, not seeking my own advantage, but that of many, that they may be saved.*
> *- 1 Corinthians 10:31-33*

Considering the conscience of the other person, whether or not they are lost and ignorant of God's ways or whether they have been enlightened by knowledge, is part of how we exalt or elevate God in all things! Remember, part of glorifying God is making Him look good in the eyes of the weak or lost. The goal is not to achieve some technical state of righteousness but to do all we can "that they may be saved." Which means my mother was right, of course. Regardless of whether or not my girlfriend and I actually pursued sexual activity, if I put myself in a position where my friends thought it happened, it would damage my ability to influence them for the gospel! And because they all knew that I professed to be a Christian, it would diminish their view of my faith and the Church if they even *perceived* that I was simply acting like any other person. I needed to hold myself to a standard that could not be impeached by their ignorance!

There are many situations this principle could apply to, places or activities or behaviors that might not be explicitly condemned in scripture but could nevertheless be misunderstood or give an opening to those who want to disparage our character as Christians. In this way these things would become sinful, by hampering our ability to be the light of the world. How often do you think about how your behavior could be twisted or your influence compromised?

Avoiding Actual Evil

Of course, we do actually have to act righteously, right? It's good to avoid "the appearance" of evil, but you first need to avoid literal evil! We must stand apart from sinful behavior.

> *Since therefore Christ suffered in the flesh, arm yourselves with the same way of thinking, for whoever has suffered in the flesh has ceased from sin, so as to live for the rest of the time in the flesh no longer for human passions but for the will of God. For the time that is past suffices for doing what the Gentiles want to do, living in sensuality, passions, drunkenness, orgies, drinking parties, and lawless idolatry. With respect to this they are surprised when you do not join them in the same flood of debauchery, and they malign you; but they will give account to him who is ready to judge the living and the dead.*
>
> *- 1 Peter 4:1-5*

The goals of "give no offense" (1 Corinthians 10:32) and "ceasing from sin" (1 Peter 4:1) are sometimes at odds with one another. Sometimes, the lost we associate with (through work, school, friendship, or even family bonds) will want to participate in sinful things, and we will need to refuse. Often when we do so it *will* give offense, no matter how we bow out. God is clear that "ceasing from sin" takes priority over "give no offense."

But even as we refuse to participate in sinful activity, we need to be thoughtful about how we excuse ourselves from situations that could lead to sinful behavior. We need to be aware of how we portray our desire to be holy. Are we self-righteous about our holiness? Are we derogatory of their wickedness? Or do we have Paul's attitude of desperately wanting to help the lost? Are we arrogant in our righteousness or sad over their ignorance? How we respond when we are mistreated for trying to live holy lives matters a great deal!

> *Bless those who persecute you; bless and do not curse them. Rejoice with those who rejoice, weep with those who weep. Live in harmony with one another. Do not be haughty, but associate with the lowly. Never be wise in your own sight. Repay no one evil for evil, but give thought to do what is honorable in the sight of all. If possible, so far as it depends on you, live peaceably with all. Beloved, never avenge yourselves, but leave it to the wrath of God, for it is written, "Vengeance is mine, I will repay, says the Lord." To the contrary, "if your enemy is hungry, feed him; if he is thirsty, give him something to drink; for by so doing you will heap burning coals on his head." Do not be overcome by evil, but overcome evil with good.*
>
> *- Romans 12:14-21*

In all circumstances, we bear the responsibility of treating the other person righteously. We never have an excuse to respond in kind to our mistreatment. It can take a great deal of self-control to refrain from seeking vengeance.

Oh how hard it can be to leave it to the wrath of God! Balancing holy separation from sin with the need to give no offense to anyone is a difficult task! Sometimes, no matter how thoughtful or intentional we are, our refusal to participate in sin *will* result in maligning or mistreatment. This is so frustrating! It can be tempting to just wash our hands of the whole thing.

WE NEED TO STAY IN THE WORLD

The temptation might be to withdraw from the world and avoid this problem altogether. If I don't interact with the lost and ignorant, they can't misconstrue and twist my behavior in order to malign me. If I don't associate with the worldly, I won't be tempted to join them in their behavior. This is the approach that several groups have taken, but we know that this attitude is not what Jesus intended:

> *I have given them your word, and the world has hated them because they are not of the world, just as I am not of the world. I do not ask that you take them out of the world, but that you keep them from the evil one. They are not of the world, just as I am not of the world. Sanctify them in the truth; your word is truth. As you sent me into the world, so I have sent them into the world.*
> - John 17:14-18

Jesus intended us to be in the world! He specifically asked God not to take his people (including us) out of the world, even though he knew they would hate us. Rather, he wanted us to be "sanctified." This means "made holy" or "set apart for holy purpose."

Paul reinforced this idea later, when he warned the church in Corinth to separate from a sinful member caught in a terrible situation:

> *I wrote to you in my letter not to associate with sexually immoral people— not at all meaning the sexually immoral of this world, or the greedy and swindlers, or idolaters, since then you would need to go out of the world.*
> - 1 Corinthians 5:9-10

It can be difficult and complicated to glorify God as we remain amid people who want to diminish God's glory, but if we remove ourselves from the world, who will glorify God? Who will maintain the light of His awesomeness? As Jesus instructed very early in his ministry:

> *You are the salt of the earth, but if salt has lost its taste, how shall its saltiness be restored? It is no longer good for anything except to be thrown out and trampled under people's feet.*
>
> *You are the light of the world. A city set on a hill cannot be hidden. Nor do people light a lamp and put it under a basket, but on a stand, and it gives light to all in the house. In the same way, let your light shine before others, so that they may see your good works and give glory to your Father who is in heaven.*
> - Matthew 5:13-16

This is not an optional extra; it is an explicit command. Jesus very clearly wants us to be visible and involved in the world. Salt is designed to season. It doesn't do any good left in the container: it has to touch and mingle with the food! He specifically told us not to hide ourselves away ("under a basket" in the text). If we are to be the light of the world, the world has to be able to see us.

A DIFFICULT TASK

God has given us a difficult task that requires wisdom and discernment. We need to stay in the world and associate with the lost, while avoiding sin, and also doing all we can to give offense to no one, including the lost. We need to not just avoid sinful actions but even situations that might appear to be evil, or misunderstood to be evil. But we still need to interact with the lost; else, how will they see God?

> *But rejoice insofar as you share Christ's sufferings, that you may also rejoice and be glad when his glory is revealed. If you are insulted for the name of Christ, you are blessed, because the Spirit of glory and of God rests upon you. But let none of you suffer as a murderer or a thief or an evildoer or as a meddler. Yet if anyone suffers as a Christian, let him not be ashamed, but let him glorify God in that name.*
>
> *- 1 Peter 4:13-16*

There are a lot of conflicting emotions when dealing with the lost. On the one hand, when we are mistreated for refusing to conform to the world's standard, we should rejoice, because that is a sign that we share in Christ! But there should also be sadness for the lostness of the world (Romans 9:1-2), anger at the rebellion of God's creation, and urgency to teach all we can. If we are not careful, we can be swung too far along these axes by focusing too much on one emotional response.

Our anger at the world's rejection of Jesus might lead us to arrogance and exclusivity: *I want to keep those people out of God's kingdom for the way they treat us.*

Our empathy and compassion might lead us to compromise the truth: *We just want everyone to love God and each other, so why not relax some of God's more onerous commands?*

Our sadness might lead us to despair and despondency: *What's the point of trying to evangelize if no one is going to convert?*

These are all sinful reactions!

It takes wisdom to know how to balance these competing motivations...

> *Walk in wisdom toward outsiders, making the best use of the time. Let your speech always be gracious, seasoned with salt, so that you may know how you ought to answer each person.*
> *- Colossians 4:5-6*

> *If any of you lacks wisdom, let him ask God, who gives generously to all without reproach, and it will be given him. But let him ask in faith, with no doubting, for the one who doubts is like a wave of the sea that is driven and tossed by the wind.*
> *- James 1:5-6*

> *...for everyone who lives on milk is unskilled in the word of righteousness, since he is a child. But solid food is for the mature, for those who have their powers of discernment trained by constant practice to distinguish good from evil.*
> *- Hebrews 5:13-14*

Knowing how to appropriately respond to and relate to the lost, especially when they want us to join them in sin and react badly when we don't, is a skill that can be developed. It requires the wisdom that God can and wants to give us. It requires practice and training. Nobody is born knowing how to do this. And, like so many things, it requires the help of the church, seeking the counsel of wiser, more experienced Christians. This is part of why we need to be a part of a congregation. If you aren't sure how to balance these competing goals, seek guidance and help! Are we availing ourselves of every avenue of aid?

Let's End with Some Catchy Acronyms

I don't usually use this sort of thing, but I find these acronyms and questions to be particularly useful in trying to live out Biblical principles. Before you act:

THINK (version 1): Is it **T**rue? Is it **H**urtful? Is it **I**llegal? Is it **N**ecessary? Is it **K**ind?

THINK (version 2): Is it **T**rue? Is it **H**urtful? Is it **I**nspiring? Is it **N**ecessary? Is it **K**ind?

BRAIN: What are the **B**enefits? What are the **R**isks? What are the **A**lternatives? What does my **I**ntuition tell me? What if I do **N**othing?

BREW: Is it **B**iblical? Is it **R**esponsible? Is it **E**difying? Is it **W**ise?

Digging Deeper

1. How often do you consider what a non-Christian would think of your behavior? What are some things you regularly do that might be easily misunderstood by those who aren't familiar with God or the Bible?

2. List some things that are worth doing or attitudes that are worth having even though people in the world will probably misunderstand them. What evidence do you have that God views these things the same way?

3. Are there things you would do or say in the company of mature Christians that you wouldn't around younger or weaker Christians? Why or why not? What are some of these things?

4. Are you ever tempted to avoid interacting with those outside the church? If so, why? What is the danger in this temptation?

7. Glory in the World, Part 2: The Importance of Holy Identity

More discussion is necessary about how to glorify God while living in a fallen world. Remember, the point is to elevate and please the Lord, not ourselves. How do we make Him look? How do we point others to Him? How is He praised by what we do, say, and think?

The struggle highlighted in the previous chapter comes from the fact that we, as citizens of God's kingdom, still have to live on earth and interact with people who want nothing to do with God. How do we maintain our holiness in the world, while also engaging with the lost? How do we bring as much glory to God as possible, while also striving to become "all things to all men"?

We have examined some of God's instructions for us in this matter; but now let us zero in on one key concept: *identity*. Who are we? What makes us who we are? What are the most important things to us? How do we think about ourselves? These are questions of identity, and how we answer these questions will directly impact our ability to glorify God.

Let me be as clear as I can: a lot of the reason we fail to glorify God is that we identify ourselves using the wrong things or we place the wrong things at the core of our self-identity. Everyone belongs to many groups. Your surname is a marker of identity; so is your nationality, your race, your gender, your job, and your place in the family. Your unique combination of all the various aspects of human experience and endeavor adds up to form who you are. But there should be one component of our being that matters more than all the others:

> *Beloved, I urge you as sojourners and exiles to abstain from the passions of the flesh, which wage war against your soul.*
> - 1 Peter 2:11

We have read this verse so many times already, but it bears repeating: where have we been exiled from? What does the word "sojourner" mean? Paul perhaps makes it clearer:

> *For many, of whom I have often told you and now tell you even with tears, walk as enemies of the cross of Christ. Their end is destruction, their god is their belly, and they glory in their shame, with minds set on earthly things. But our citizenship is in heaven, and from it we await a Savior, the Lord Jesus Christ, who will transform our lowly body to be like his glorious body, by the power that enables him even to subject all things to himself.*
> - Philippians 3:18-21

But our citizenship is in heaven. We belong with God. That is our primary home. We sojourn on the earth for a time, but we do not truly belong here! The more we "set our minds on earthly things," the more we will forget this truth. Thinking that this world is where we belong, instead of a temporary location, leads to spiritual destruction and death, eternal separation from God.

> *Share in suffering as a good soldier of Christ Jesus. No soldier gets entangled in civilian pursuits, since his aim is to please the one who enlisted him.*
> - 2 Timothy 2:3-4

The almighty God has called us out of this world and enlisted us in a spiritual army. We are on tour in the world, away from our home nation. We must not become entangled in the civilian pursuits of the earthly nation we happen to be in. When these pursuits become more important to us than godly things, we will inevitably stop pleasing the One who enlisted us.

What are some of these pursuits? Put another way, what are the ways we confuse and compromise our identity? What are some of the "earthly things" that we get entangled with? To be sure, there are many, but for our purposes I want to highlight three main categories.

Personal Politics

We are going to discuss this in more detail in a later chapter, but I want to touch on this briefly: your political affiliation should matter less to your identity than your spiritual affiliation! If you spend more time thinking about politics than you do thinking about spiritual matters, you are almost certainly confusing your identity. Jesus and the apostles were almost entirely apolitical. It's not right to say they didn't talk about politics, because they did, a bit. But what did they say? Obey the government (Romans 13:1-7, Titus 3:1-11); pay your taxes (Matthew 22:15-22); pray for earthly rulers (1 Timothy 2:1-4); and seek a quiet, peaceful life (1 Timothy 2:2). The early Church was not politically active nor were they politically revolutionary.

If you let a person's political beliefs (those that don't overlap with explicit commands of God for His people) affect your relationship with them, you are sinning.

Politics are the epitome of "earthly things" (Philippians 3:19). Consider:

> *Let every person be subject to the governing authorities. For there is no authority except from God, and those that exist have been instituted by God. Therefore whoever resists the authorities resists what God has appointed, and those who resist will incur judgment.*
>
> *- Romans 13:1-2*

If you are a "conservative," I hope you didn't use this verse to support Trump if you aren't using it to support Biden. If you are a "liberal," are you suddenly pulling this verse out of the closet after ignoring it for four years? Don't preach Romans 13 when your guy wins and Revelation 13 (the sign of the beast) when the other guy wins. This is exactly the kind of behavior Peter warned us not to engage in when he said that the ignorant twist Scripture to their own destruction (2 Peter 3:16).

Are there aspects of politics that touch on matters of righteousness? Of course there are! But in those areas, you should believe what you believe because of what the Bible says, not because it's the party line. Even where there are disagreements in the Church about political issues that truly matter, *we should not be approaching them as political issues*. If they matter from a spiritual perspective, we should handle them as such, instead of considering them politically. Don't confuse matters of righteousness as matters of politics!

About this there is much to say, and it will be said in a later chapter, but for now, meditate on this: *our citizenship is in heaven*. If you care more about the earthly kingdom you live in than the heavenly kingdom you belong to, you might not actually belong in the heavenly kingdom at all!

You are a Christian first, then probably a member of your physical family second, then maybe a member of your political party third or fourth. When we place our earthly citizenship first in our hearts and minds, who will we glorify? It won't be God, will it? The glory of your nation is secondary to God's glory!

Cultural Differences

The concepts of government, nationality, and culture are all closely intertwined, though they are separate. The country I live in (the USA) was conceived of as a "melting pot," a place where multiple cultures would mix in a giant conglomeration.

America was not the first to do this. The Romans did this long before; they created a grand empire spanning multiple continents. They allowed each conquered nation to retain most of their culture under Roman rule; this is why the Jews continued to offer sacrifices and follow the Law of Moses, while the Gentiles continued to worship Artemis and Zeus and the rest of the Greco-Roman pantheon.

The importance people place on these kinds of cultural and national identity became a source of great contention in the early Church. For the first time in history, the Kingdom of God was spreading far beyond the confines of the one isolated nation that had been the center of it for so long under the old covenant (Israel).

> *Now in these days when the disciples were increasing in number, a complaint by the Hellenists*

> *arose against the Hebrews because their widows were being neglected in the daily distribution.*
> *- Acts 6:1*

This is very early in the Church's history! That word "Hellenists" means "Greek-speaking Jews." This wasn't even a matter of racism (they were all Jews), it was just a matter of speaking a different language (personal history and culture). They allowed this cultural difference to cause a real rift, eventually requiring the call of very specific, gifted men to resolve (Acts 6:1-7). Later, we see:

> *Now those who were scattered because of the persecution that arose over Stephen traveled as far as Phoenicia and Cyprus and Antioch, speaking the word to no one except Jews.*
> *- Acts 11:19*

As the Jews travelled out of the confines of Judea, they still couldn't move past their own nation and culture, even though the previous chapter (Acts 10) made clear that God intended to include people of all nationalities in the Kingdom.

Why would the Jews keep excluding non-Jews? Maybe they were more comfortable with their own people? Maybe they were afraid of the language barrier? Or maybe they were explicitly racist. Whatever the reason, the result was the same: people of different nationalities were not getting a fair shot at repentance! This could have cost people eternal salvation!

> *There is neither Jew nor Greek, there is neither slave nor free, there is no male and female, for you are all one in Christ Jesus. And if you are Christ's, then you are Abraham's offspring, heirs according to promise.*
> *- Galatians 3:28-29*

There are so many things we humans use to divide and categorize ourselves: race, language, customs, etc. But all of these things are secondary or tertiary to what really matters: do we belong to Christ? I may be white, but that marker of my identity is eternally useless and should not factor into my attempts to glorify God. If racial differences do not matter in heaven, they should not matter in God's kingdom on earth (the Church):

> *From now on, therefore, we regard no one according to the flesh. Even though we once regarded Christ according to the flesh, we regard him thus no longer. Therefore, if anyone is in Christ, he is a new creation. The old has passed away; behold, the new has come. All this is from God, who through Christ reconciled us to himself and gave us the ministry of reconciliation; that is, in Christ God was reconciling the world to himself, not counting their trespasses against them, and entrusting to us the message of reconciliation.*
> - 2 Corinthians 5:16-19

People may speak different languages or dress differently or eat different things or be a different color, but it is sinful to use those differences to divide the Church and thus diminish God's glory. These are, again, the very definition of "earthly things" in Philippians 3. Or, as Paul says in 2 Corinthians 5, these are matters of "the flesh," attributes that we should not be using as criteria to regard or evaluate one another any longer.

So, if you feel like "your way of life" is threatened by the presence of those who do not eat, talk, or act like you, so what? Do you care more about keeping your cultural identity than you do about the opportunity to evangelize to or have Christian fellowship with more people?

Family Ties

Finally, consider the other primary way the world classifies identity: your family. What did Christ have to say about that?

> *While he was still speaking to the people, behold, his mother and his brothers stood outside, asking to speak to him. But he replied to the man who told him, "Who is my mother, and who are my brothers?" And stretching out his hand toward his disciples, he said, "Here are my mother and my brothers! For whoever does the will of my Father in heaven is my brother and sister and mother."*
>
> *- Matthew 12:46-50*

If you have an earthly family that is part of the Kingdom of God, great! But many, many people do not, and they have to make a supremely difficult choice to forsake father and mother for the sake of Christ. Do not make them feel like outsiders through neglect or judgment or ungraciousness or partiality!

God intended for such people to find a new, better family; if we want to glorify God, we will adjust our sense of familial identity accordingly. These are the people we will spend eternity with! These are our fellow soldiers, our fellow workers, our mentors, our children, our helpers, and our co-inheritors of eternal life! These are the people with whom we should share a common goal and mission. These are the people who will help us glorify God!

Putting it All Together

I am a straight, white, mostly apolitical American male in

the 18-34 demographic who speaks English and comes from wherever it is my family comes from (I really don't know, and that's okay). These are things the world uses to classify and identify me; this is my demographic. This is the box the world will try to put me in and keep me in.

It is tempting to allow these things to influence my behavior and who I associate with. Maybe I should do what everyone else in my demo is doing? Maybe I should hate people who have different political opinions or who come from a different nation or who are a different color or who are older or younger? Doesn't it seem like the world wants us to do this, to divide ourselves along demographic lines?

But these classifications are eternally meaningless. They are fleshly and earthly, not spiritual:

> *Now we have received not the spirit of the world, but the Spirit who is from God, that we might understand the things freely given us by God. And we impart this in words not taught by human wisdom but taught by the Spirit, interpreting spiritual truths to those who are spiritual. The natural person does not accept the things of the Spirit of God, for they are folly to him, and he is not able to understand them because they are spiritually discerned.*
>
> *- 1 Corinthians 2:12-14*

It will be (and should be!) strange to the world that we don't care about the same things they do and don't identify ourselves using the same markers they do. That's the whole point! Be strange, be different, identify as a Christian above and beyond anything else!

That means that we should critically examine political issues according to God's standard, not the standard of a specific party. The idea that either of the major parties in

America is perfectly aligned with God's standard is laughable! It means we should evaluate cultural issues separately from doctrinal ones: God is clear about what He wants and silent about so much that He obviously doesn't care about. We must continually be careful not to presume to know better than God what He wants and not overstep in pronouncing judgment over things that God has given no indication He will judge.

We must stop evaluating (regarding) people based on skin color or nationality or dress or eating habits. Allowing the world to dictate our identity only leads to dishonor, not glory. God's kingdom will not expand, God's light will not shine, if we allow the world to trick and trap us in these false boxes. We are supposed to be different from the world, so let's start thinking and acting differently from the world!

Digging Deeper

1. What aspects of yourself (looks, abilities, interests, or something else) do you consider to be the most important parts of your identity? Why those, and not the rest of the things that make you unique?

2. What aspects of other people (looks, abilities, interests, politics, etc.) are most important to you? What parts of their personas most influence how you treat them?

3. What sorts of things do you spend the most time thinking about or participating in (other than work and sleep)? If the answer is not "spiritual things", why is that?

4. How does the concept of "personal identity" contribute to the pursuit of *meaning* we discussed in chapter 1? Why does this matter?

8. Glory through Sex: Confronting the World with God's Glory

The year is 2080, and the church needs new deacons. There is a particularly well-respected man at church, one converted in his 20s, who has been faithful and diligent, has a loving wife and three adopted children (they felt adoption is a needed ministry in the world). So, naturally, this man is selected to be a deacon. He serves faithfully for several years.

In the course of things, through time and chance, a shocking truth is revealed: this man was born as a woman! Early in his (her? their?) life, they underwent therapy and surgery to become what they knew themselves to be in their hearts (I'm going to use "they" for the rest of this section, as an example of what our language may look like in 60 years). Because of the nature of gender discussion in society, almost everyone they knew just accepted it. For all practical purposes, they really became male, in both physicality (because medical technology advanced to the point of making this possible) and in social dynamic. From their late teens onward, it was never discussed again, and they lived life wholly as a man. They went to college and met their spouse, who never knew of the change. Why would she? This is an accepted, normal part of life! Even asking about such things is insensitive and bigoted, so, of course, she wouldn't have thought to inquire. She, like a well-adjusted member of society, accepted at face-value what her date presented himself as.

After college, they adopted three children from a poverty-stricken country. They lived their lives. They were, through the hard work of a local church, converted to Christ, and thus we return to the beginning of our story. At this juncture, several questions present themselves.

- What is this person's responsibility toward their spouse of 20 years?
- What is this person's responsibility toward their children (ages 16, 14, and 12) whom they have been raising diligently and faithfully "in the Lord" ever since their spiritual conversion?
- What if the gender conversion had never been revealed, and no one had ever known?

One might think: *surely if this person had been converted to Christ, they would have felt compelled to disclose this as a matter of righteousness*! But why would they? The Bible speaks of the roles of men and women, which this person could easily have accepted and adopted; but it speaks nothing of men becoming women. When the Bible was written, it wasn't possible for men to become women in any real or complete way! We could even reverse this scenario; a person is born as a man, becomes a female, and post-conversion accepts the teaching of Scripture about gender authority and submits to male spiritual leadership. That person would think they were doing the righteous thing, because, of course, they are female (in their mind at least). This scenario might seem far-fetched to you now, but it won't be to future generations, so now is the time to start thinking about and planning for what we will teach our children.

It is very difficult to confront our most basic beliefs; the things we think are so blatantly, obviously true that we would never even articulate them out loud, let alone question them. Why would a person who has for their whole lives accepted a certain worldview ever question the reality of that narrative? When converted to a belief in the Bible, they would read the passages that discuss men and women and group themselves in with the gender they have identified with and become. They would likely never feel the need to disclose something that, in their minds, isn't relevant to Christianity, because the Bible never discusses it!

This example is an extreme one, yes, and potentially one your congregation will never face. But, if it did, what would you say to such a person? What would you advise them (Him? Her? Seriously, which word would you use?) to do for themselves, their family, and for God? More importantly, what scriptures would you use to support your advice? What would be the God-glorifying path forward for that person, their family, and the church?

Sexuality: The Core of Modern Identity

One cannot spend any time immersed in popular culture and not realize the importance the world places on sexual identity. Perhaps more than any other marker, gender and sexual preference have become the pillars of a person's identity in the secular world. Additionally, sex itself has become one of the core aspects of our media, economy, and lifestyles. How many advertisements, shows, and products use sexuality as a defining trait? Here's a few astonishing statistics, courtesy of Psychology Today: porn websites get more internet traffic than Netflix, Amazon, and Twitter combined. 30% of all data passed along the internet is porn related. It is an estimated $100 billion industry, and that is just the explicit stuff! What about all the content that isn't explicitly sexual but still uses sexuality as one of its primary hooks?

The last 50 years have seen a dramatic change in the perceptions of sex and gender, but most of these changes aren't really changes at all. People have always rebelled against God's intent for human sexuality, which is why the Bible talks a lot about righteous and unrighteous sexual expression:

> *Therefore a man shall leave his father and his mother and hold fast to his wife, and they shall become one flesh. And the man and his wife were both naked and were not ashamed.*
> *- Genesis 2:24-25*

This was before any sin entered the world, so we know that sex is not inherently wrong. It was part of God's original design of creation. Even after the fall, we know that sex can be righteous:

> *Let marriage be held in honor among all, and let the marriage bed be undefiled, for God will judge the sexually immoral and adulterous.*
> *- Hebrews 13:4*

Sex, as part of God's original, untainted creation, can be glorifying to Him in the right contexts. Read the Song of Solomon sometime. Sex is both the God-given means of procreation and a God-given avenue of pleasure, when done in a holy way. Of course, the problem is the ways we defile this part of God's creation, right? For the most part, 21st century Americans haven't figured out any new way to do that:

> *For this reason God gave them up to dishonorable passions. For their women exchanged natural relations for those that are contrary to nature; and the men likewise gave up natural relations with women and were consumed with passion for one another, men committing shameless acts with men and receiving in themselves the due penalty for their error.*
> *- Romans 1:26-27*

This might have been written to a church today! We shouldn't think that we are in some way special; we aren't any more or less wicked than any past group of people. Humanity always finds ways to live contrary to God's established creation.

Our particular problem is the way sexuality has become so important to who we are as individuals. Our preferences have become one of the primary ways we group and segregate ourselves. Like political affiliations, cultural heritage, or family ties, sexuality can easily take the place of Christ as the foundation of our identity. Consider the acronym LGBTQ+, which stands for Lesbian, Gay, Bisexual, Transgender, Queer, and more. For many people who identify as one or more of these, this is the core of their identity! When we talk with people about what the Bible says about these things, it will sound the same way it would if we were telling people their family are all a bunch of liars, murderers, and thieves, or if we disparaged their life's work. These are deeply held parts of a person's psyche!

Often, attempts to talk about these things, even with the

best intentions, come across as condemnation of a person's very existence (not just behavior or lifestyle). This is true even if we take the utmost care with our words and attitudes. Imagine how it will be if we are careless!

I am worried that the Church is not equipped to handle this issue in a way that glorifies God. We might certainly condemn, speak out against, or decry the new gender theory or sexual revolution, but how do we follow Paul's instructions to the Colossians?

> *Walk in wisdom toward outsiders, making the best use of the time. Let your speech always be gracious, seasoned with salt, so that you may know how you ought to answer each person.*
> - Colossians 4:5-6

It's one thing to know what you believe to be true; it's another to know how to say it wisely, graciously, and beneficially. So, the crux of this chapter: what does the world say about gender and sex, and what does the Bible say; and, how do we approach this topic in a way that both glorifies God and reaches the lost?

THE NEW SCIENCE OF GENDER

This is a difficult thing to discuss in a productive way, because I imagine many of my readers will think something like, "Well, this is stupid! Of course there are only two genders! Anyone can clearly see that! Look at biology!" As we have said, it is extremely difficult to confront the beliefs we hold to be obviously self-evident, so blatantly true that we have never once thought the world could be any other way. Because of this, it is going to be hard for many Christians to effectively minister to members of the LGBTQ+ community;

not because we will be tempted to compromise, but because we have no common frame of reference with which to communicate.

I'm going to spend a little time trying to explain the new gender and sexual theory. Do not misunderstand; I am not saying that I agree with what I am about to say, but if we cannot understand the way the world thinks on this subject, I do not think we will be able to reach them with the gospel. I guess we could just ignore this section of the population and write them off entirely, but does that seem righteous to you? Does that sound like something Christ, who literally left heaven to call the lost, would do?

It's hard to pin down any standard, unified set of new gender beliefs because the ideology is still in its formative stage. If you Google "How many genders are there?" you will get answers ranging from the low teens to the high sixties, but really, that's not how a lot of the world thinks about gender anymore. To many, gender is not an either/or, but is instead a spectrum. To much of the world, it is a gradient on which you could find yourself at any of a thousand points. Fundamentally, the transgender movement rejects the idea that gender is something based in biology and embraces the idea that gender is entirely (or at least mostly) a social construct. "Male" and "female" are now things dictated by societal norms, not by what reproductive organs you have.

Even as I write this, I can feel some of my readers tuning out in confusion and disdain, but please try to understand. These are eternal souls, created in the image of God, currently bound for eternal condemnation. Does God love them any less because they are confused and lost? Should we? Never before has 2 Corinthians 4 meant more to me:

> *And even if our gospel is veiled, it is veiled to those who are perishing. In their case the god of this world*

has blinded the minds of the unbelievers, to keep them from seeing the light of the gospel of the glory of Christ, who is the image of God.
- 2 Corinthians 4:3-4

Satan has blinded this world! He has kept them from seeing God's glory! In this case, he has specifically kept them from seeing the glory of God's intent for creation. It is our job to help illuminate the truth to those he has deceived! Step one is understanding the deception.

At the core, this is a matter of what we believe about truth itself and where it comes from. The transgender movement is but an extension of a much older, deeper deception: that truth is relative and reality is subjective and self-determined – that individual experience and societal power structures, not Divine Imperative, determine what is true or not. It is a rejection of objective truth at the basest level. This line of thinking first led to moral relativism and the rejection of absolute morality. It is not a stretch to imagine this would lead to a rejection of biological determinism.

As we approach this topic, we must do so with the understanding that arguing from biology or nature is like arguing the finer points of doctrine with an atheist. There are more fundamental things to consider before we start debating the practical matters of theology.

Please understand: many people have divorced the concepts of biological sex from gender. They have redefined what the word *gender* means. Under this new paradigm, *sex* is the thing determined by DNA, chromosomes, and reproductive organs; *gender* is a complex amalgam of societal expectations, roles, definitions, and self-expression. Supposedly, gender is imposed upon us by the expectations of the world, not necessarily by the "accident" of birth. To be clear, even the most ardent defenders of transgenderism understand that for most people, gender and sex will align. The question, as always, is what about the rare exceptions?

A FIRST WORLD PROBLEM

It would be easy, or at least easier, if the Bible said something like "Thou shalt not change thy gender." But it doesn't, because up until quite recently, it wasn't really a possibility. Imagine if God had put this kind of language or command in scripture. How nonsensical it would have sounded to the original readers! Technology and the extravagant affluence of our society have made this debate even possible. These sorts of debates and ideas don't occur in places where you must worry about your next meal. Why would you ever question the nature of sexual biology when your society is crumbling around you? We have been at such a high level of wealth for so long that people feel compelled to find new things to question and struggle with, new battles to fight, new rules and expectations to rebel against. And, we have finally reached a level of personal wealth where spending money on such a thing is feasible.

Additionally, the Bible doesn't say anything explicit about gender being the same thing as biological sex, because for most of history, people couldn't imagine it being any different, that there might be any other way for it to be! So, while sexual sin has been a problem since almost the very beginning, because it was always within the reach of humanity, this new gender theory simply wasn't feasible before now. However, it's here now and we need to deal with it.

How we deal with it is a two-part process: First, we must understand what the Bible says about sex and gender, and then we must think about how we righteously convey that information to the world.

SO, WHAT DOES THE BIBLE SAY?

> *For many, of whom I have often told you and now tell you even with tears, walk as enemies of the cross of Christ. Their end is destruction, their god is their belly, and they glory in their shame, with minds set on earthly things.*
> - Philippians 3:18-19

This passage is apt in such a discussion. Many people in the world *do* glory in things that are shameful, things that are simply gratifications of the flesh. This issue, like so many others, is a matter of gratifying the flesh. However, we must be exceedingly careful about our attitudes!

Paul talked of these people "with tears." Disgust, disdain, or dismissal – these are perhaps common responses to the new gender paradigm, but it is very easy for us to be unrighteous in our attitude and behavior. Do you feel any sadness that so many people will be lost because of their confusion over things like homosexuality and transgenderism? How do we talk about these things? What scriptures should we or can we use in such discussions?

From the very beginning of creation, God had an intended pattern for humanity. He made us with a particular function and purpose, and included sexuality as part of His design from a time before sin entered the world:

> *Then God said, "Let us make man in our image, after our likeness. And let them have dominion over the fish of the sea and over the birds of the heavens and over the livestock and over all the earth and over every*

> *creeping thing that creeps on the earth."*
> *So God created man in his own image,*
> *in the image of God he created him;*
> *male and female he created them.*
> — Genesis 1:26-27

> *Then the man said,*
> *"This at last is bone of my bones*
> *and flesh of my flesh;*
> *she shall be called Woman,*
> *because she was taken out of Man."*
> *Therefore a man shall leave his father and his mother and hold fast to his wife, and they shall become one flesh. And the man and his wife were both naked and were not ashamed.*
> — Genesis 2:23-25

This is the intention of God, prior to any sin or wickedness: the separation of the genders and the sexual relationship between them for life. Deviation from this model, both in sexual preference and number of sexual partners, is condemned in both the Mosaic Covenant and the Covenant of Christ (Leviticus 18:22, Malachi 2:13-16, Matthew 19:1-9). These are principles that transcend specific covenantal laws.

But if you believe in your heart of hearts that gender and sex aren't the same thing and that gender is just a social construct, what will these Scriptures mean to you? We could read passage after passage (1 Corinthians 11:2-16, 1 Corinthians 14:33-37, 1 Timothy 2:8-15, 1 Peter 3:1-7) about the assigned gender roles in the covenant of Christ, but what will that mean? Even some Christians teach that yes, all these passages might be true, but your sex isn't what determines if you read these as "male" or "female"; your self-identified gender does. How would you respond to that?

First, consider the idea of "submission." We are told in numerous places that we need to submit to God's will. Part of that will, outlined in Scripture, is the prescribed roles and responsibilities of each gender. Scripture approaches the matter like this: You are whatever you are born as (male or female), and so this is the role or behavior that is expected of you.

Swapping genders is not submitting to the standard God assigned. It is a means of side-stepping that standard. The new gender ideology says, "If you don't feel like you are male, that means you aren't male." Can you imagine how Paul would respond if someone said, "I don't feel in my heart of hearts that I should be female, so I am not going to submit to the role God has assigned to females"? Do you think Peter or any of the apostles would have accepted this as a reasonable excuse?

The Bible is not silent about using "nature" as a general guidepost for figuring out what is real, right, or wrong. Return to a passage we read previously:

> *For this reason God gave them up to dishonorable passions. For their women exchanged natural relations for those that are contrary to nature; and the men likewise gave up natural relations with women and were consumed with passion for one another, men committing shameless acts with men and receiving in themselves the due penalty for their error.*
> *- Romans 1:26-27*

Paul's argument against homosexuality (which is backed up in other places with different kinds of arguments, see 1 Corinthians 6:9-10, 1 Timothy 1:8-11) is based in the "natural relations." He specifically calls it wicked behavior because it is that which is "contrary to nature." Paul seems to think that (at least in this instance) nature has something to do with morality. He uses the same sort of argument in another place:

> *Judge for yourselves: is it proper for a wife to pray to God with her head uncovered? Does not nature itself teach you that if a man wears long hair it is a disgrace for him, but if a woman has long hair, it is her glory? For her hair is given to her for a covering. If anyone is inclined to be contentious, we have no such practice, nor do the churches of God.*
> *- 1 Corinthians 11:13-16*

"Does not nature itself teach you..." is a very telling phrase. Now, in this case, Paul didn't think the matter important enough to enforce if anyone was "inclined to be contentious," whereas in the matters of homosexuality he clearly did think it needed to be enforced. Consider one more passage:

> *For when Gentiles, who do not have the law, by nature do what the law requires, they are a law to themselves, even though they do not have the law. They show that the work of the law is written on their hearts, while their conscience also bears witness, and their conflicting thoughts accuse or even excuse them on that day when, according to my gospel, God judges the secrets of men by Christ Jesus.*
> *- Romans 2:14-16*

How did the Gentiles do what the law required? They had some part of that law, some fundamental morality, embedded in their "nature." They didn't have to do anything to acquire it – it was just there.

So, what is the point? Nature does indicate to us in some ways what is real, right, and righteous. We can see a lot of

God's intent and order for His creation in the way things have been made, including God's intended design for sex and gender. The original design of human gender and sex existed prior to sin, therefore it cannot be something wrong or unrighteous. Of course, God's original design has been corrupted by sin, and so there are times when scripture uses the term "natural" to mean something very different.

THE FLESH V. THE SPIRIT

Why do some people feel attracted to the same sex? It's not always just a conscious choice; human sexuality has a large psychological and physiological component you can't just turn on or off like a switch, but we could say the same of any number of other sinful behaviors. Why are some people more susceptible to alcoholism? Why are some people more prone to anger? Sin is always a choice, of course, but *temptation* often has a genetic or physiological component outside of our control! Some temptations come from the deepest parts of the flesh and can be different from person to person! Ultimately, the Bible offers the same guidance in each of these cases:

> *The night is far gone; the day is at hand. So then let us cast off the works of darkness and put on the armor of light. Let us walk properly as in the daytime, not in orgies and drunkenness, not in sexual immorality and sensuality, not in quarreling and jealousy. But put on the Lord Jesus Christ, and make no provision for the flesh, to gratify its desires.*
> - Romans 13:12-14

> *But I say, walk by the Spirit, and you will not gratify the desires of the flesh. For the desires of the flesh*

> *are against the Spirit, and the desires of the Spirit are against the flesh, for these are opposed to each other, to keep you from doing the things you want to do.*
> — Galatians 5:16-17

When we try to present God's moral standard for human sexuality, the objection is often, *why would God make me this way if He didn't want me to live this way?* The answer is obvious: the flesh, the things we feel in our bodies, including many of the emotions we feel and the deepest desires of our heart, are not always in harmony with God (Jeremiah 17:9)! We feel many things that aren't righteous; unrighteous sexual desires come from the same place as unrighteous desires for quarreling and jealousy. The flesh is against the spirit! Therefore, feelings of homosexual desire or feelings of gender dysphoria (the technical medical term for feeling like you psychologically aren't the right gender), could both be very real feelings. These feelings could even be based in biology or physiology but still be against God's will.

Our society equates happiness with physical and mental pleasure. Happiness = the gratification of the flesh. It's why even Christians sometimes pursue adultery, lying, or homosexuality, because we have misunderstood God's highest priority. God doesn't put our happiness at the highest priority. Our righteousness is God's greatest concern. His glory is more important than our happiness.

Thus, it seems like two contradictory things are both true: Some natural parts of God's creation speak to moral truth (Romans 1:26-27, 2:14-16, 1 Corinthians 11:13-16), and some parts do not (Romans 13:12-14, Galatians 5:16-17). How can we tell the difference? Which parts of nature are in harmony with God's will and which aren't? The only way we could know would be if God told us which natural desires are right and which ones are wrong. Fortunately, He has not been silent about the matter and has given us the scriptures we have read (and many others) to guide us through these complex questions!

God created people "male and female" and established a certain mode of sexuality in the garden, a perfect version of physical reality. Then He consistently, across multiple covenants and modes of righteousness, reinforced that original intent. He inspired prophets to use the "natural" mode of existence as evidence against engaging in sexuality in ways contrary to it. Finally, He consistently expects people to operate according to their gender, submitting to the roles He has assigned, instead of attempting to break out of the pattern He has created. Thus, our call is to submit to the model of human sexuality that God created us for.

Responding with God's Glory

So how do we help people who are struggling with the new sexual and gender paradigms? Here are some things to consider:

> *And the Lord's servant must not be quarrelsome but kind to everyone, able to teach, patiently enduring evil, correcting his opponents with gentleness. God may perhaps grant them repentance leading to a knowledge of the truth, and they may come to their senses and escape from the snare of the devil, after being captured by him to do his will.*
> *- 2 Timothy 2:24-26*

1. Stop saying that the person's feelings are invalid (or not real). We know the flesh is weak. It is very possible that they truly do feel the way they say they do, even if you can't understand it or empathize with them. Your inability to empathize does not make the other person's feelings fake or false.

2. Understand that these feelings are often some of the most deeply held beliefs about who we are. God expects everyone (the Christian and the sinner) to radically change the way we conceptualize ourselves. For many, gender and sexuality are the most central parts of who they are. Change isn't going to happen overnight! Be patient!

3. Keep your personal *feelings* to yourself. Whatever you feel about a person's lifestyle, keep the focus on what the Bible says. Attempt, to the best of your ability, to let the Bible stand on its own. The minute your discussion turns to a relative comparison of what you feel, you've lost, because you are now using the same standard of truth as the other person.

4. Be gentle. It is hard to be told that you desire unrighteous things. I'm sure every reader of this book knows that! In some cases you may be telling someone that, according to God's standard, they can never experience righteous sexual fulfillment. This is a brutal thing to hear! Consider how you say it and consider how you would feel if the positions were reversed.

5. Finally, remember, God expects everyone to sacrifice his or her own will to His:

> Then Jesus told his disciples, "If anyone would come after me, let him deny himself and take up his cross and follow me. For whoever would save his life will lose it, but whoever loses his life for my sake will find it."
> - Matthew 16:24-25

Sometimes it's impossible to change our physiology or psychology and the feelings that come from them, but we can still learn and accept that God's Word is more important. Many homosexuals will never be attracted to the opposite gender, but that doesn't mean they can't live righteously, in a way that glorifies God. Many people may feel trapped in the wrong body, like they don't belong in the gender they were born into, but they can still live out the task God has assigned to them within the parameters of gender roles God has prescribed.

Remember, the core component of our identity should not be gender, sexuality, or anything else. We are Christians above all! To suggest that a person must be able to express the desires of the flesh in order to live a fulfilled life puts the desires of the flesh at the highest priority. We are all called to sacrifice for the cross. Some of us must sacrifice "more," but in that sacrifice is an opportunity for more glory!

One of the most dangerous traps is thinking that we will always somehow reach a point where these things will never be a temptation or a trial. Sometimes, hopefully, we can, but often we just have to live with these difficulties forever. The alcoholic will always be extremely tempted and compromised by alcohol. The person who struggles with anger might always struggle with anger. Paul can certainly empathize:

> *So to keep me from becoming conceited because of the surpassing greatness of the revelations, a thorn was given me in the flesh, a messenger of Satan to harass me, to keep me from becoming conceited. Three times I pleaded with the Lord about this, that it should leave me. But he said to me, "My grace is sufficient for you, for my power is made perfect in weakness." Therefore I will boast all the more gladly of my weaknesses, so that the power of Christ may rest upon me. For the sake of Christ, then, I am content with weaknesses, insults, hardships, persecutions, and calamities. For when I am weak, then I am strong.*
> - 2 Corinthians 12:7-10

This is a book about glorifying God. Who can glorify God more than the one who is weak? It would be an exceedingly glorifying thing for people to deny what they feel in their heart of hearts, all for the sake of the gospel of Christ. Just because you don't struggle with sexual identity doesn't mean that you don't have some other difficulty that would apply in this sense. Maybe it's money, maybe you have anger issues, or you struggle with depression, or your parents are terrible. In each case, know that the power of Christ could rest upon you! If you aren't willing to sacrifice your own desires that are contrary to God, how could you possibly expect someone else to?

CONCLUSION

Let's return to the scenario at the beginning of the chapter:

• What is this person's responsibility toward their spouse of 20 years?
• What is this person's responsibility toward their children (ages 16, 14, and 12) whom they have been raising diligently and faithfully "in the Lord" ever since their conversion?
• What if the gender conversion had never been revealed and no one had ever known?

The answers are complicated and hard, aren't they? Let's start with the second one; are they still obligated to continue the job of parenting they began? Children are to be subject to both the male and female parent, so this isn't an issue of the person suddenly not having an authority they once did. They can't just cast the children out on the streets, and they can't use this as an excuse to jettison a responsibility they have from

God. On the other hand, that would mean that these children would have two mothers, according to how the Bible deals with gender. Is that okay? Is changing your gender a one-time rebellion that we are forgiven of and then remain in the state we are in? Or is it a state of rebellion that persists as long as the person remains in the new, altered state? Does one of the parents just need to stop parenting and leave the situation entirely? That doesn't seem particularly righteous considering all the numerous commands God gives to parents. We also have numerous examples of non-family members acting as mentors and guides for children that aren't their own. Maybe that's the model they should adopt? How would that look to the rest of the Church and the world?

The first question similarly has no pleasant answer. At the bare minimum, the partners should stop having sex, since their sexual activity is not within the prescribed righteous fulfillment of God's design. This is, in fact, the only part of this whole thing I feel 100% certain about. What about beyond that? If they are still obligated to parent their children, how then should that be practically accomplished? Should they get divorced or simply separate? Do they need to get a separate house? If so, where do the children live? What if they can't afford that? You can see how the mechanics of righteousness quickly become a tangled mess. It's not like they are going to stop loving their spouse that they have loved a certain way for 20 years. This isn't like a normal divorce, where the adults have no interest in each other anymore. How do you roll back the decades of commitment and dedication, the years of a shared life? This would truly be a "thorn in the flesh" for the rest of that entire family's life!

This is where the church becomes a vital part of the equation. Hopefully, the congregation that they have become a part of will be wholly committed to helping this family live righteously, to enabling holiness in a difficult situation. However, I can certainly envision how members might allow this to become a rift, potentially dividing the church.

The third question is simultaneously the easiest and the hardest to answer. God, obviously, would have known the entire time. Thankfully, judgment is His domain alone, and I don't necessarily have to have an answer for this. It is not too difficult to imagine what would happen if the gender conversion had never been revealed; they might have served faithfully as a deacon for many years, eventually become an elder, and died, all while fulfilling, to the best of their abilities, the commands of God. In that case, God alone would be the one to judge, and for that I am thankful.

This might lead us to a "don't ask, don't tell" policy, but that isn't particularly righteous, either. We have an obligation to give our best to God. Willful ignorance, while it may be easier, clearly isn't the best we can do.

Honestly, I don't have many answers in this scenario. The point of the story is to initiate thought and discussion. We, as individuals and churches, need to be thinking about these things! God clearly has a design in mind for human sexuality. If we stay within God's paradigm, it's easy; it's when we deviate that all sorts of problems begin to crop up. The new sexual and gender paradigm glorifies self above all things; thus, it is a false glory. How we respond is also a matter of glorifying Him, not just in what we say, but in how we say it. I pray that God will give us all wisdom as we strive for the gospel together.

DIGGER DEEPER

1. List some other areas where God uses the term "natural" as a guide for what is right. List some more where God uses "natural" as an indication of something wrong. In each case, what way is the word "natural" being used?

2. Why is sex so important in our culture? Do you think this is different or unique in human history? Why or why not?

3. Why is it so important to clarify terminology when we discuss gender and sex? What are some other topics where confused terminology makes the discussion harder? How can we have productive conversations about terms or definitions?

4. What are some other parts of life where God expects us to submit to His will, even though its hard or contrary to culture? In what areas of life do you find it hardest to submit to God? How can this help you in your efforts to reach the lost?

9. National Glory: When We Glorify the Wrong Thing

This chapter, like the one before, hinges on the concept of *identity*. In the previous chapter we saw that many have turned sex and sexual expression into the chief part of their self-conceptualization. Thus, it is the thing they glorify (or elevate or exalt) above all else. For many others, being an American (or whatever nationality you happen to be, dear reader) is the most important part of their identity. Sure, they aren't exalting false concepts of sex and gender, but the end result is the same: glorifying something other than the Creator.

The point of this discussion is simple, yet it will be a complicated discussion. We need to think about what we glorify or praise, both in our thoughts and in our conversations with others. What do we exalt? What do we talk about the most? What goodness do we try to convince others of more than anything else? If the answer is "America" or some version of America that we long to return to, then we might be in danger of proclaiming a false glory.

A "Christian Nation"

Let's start with this term. What many people mean when they use the term "Christian Nation" is that they want America to be a nation founded on Christian principles, populated primarily by Christians, and governed by Christians. (I am going to talk a lot about the specific context of the United States, because that is what I have the most experience with. Many of these lessons apply to Christians in other countries, of course.) The desire for most people to be Christians is a good one, but when this desire is placed in a specific geopolitical context, it can easily become sinful.

Jesus was very clear about the nature of the kingdom he was going to establish, and he talked about it on multiple occasions. This was one of the primary struggles of the disciples during Jesus' earthly ministry; people kept conceptualizing the coming kingdom as something like an earthly kingdom, only better.

Even those who didn't believe he was the Messiah, as they questioned him about his teaching, still thought this way:

> *Being asked by the Pharisees when the kingdom of God would come, he answered them, "The kingdom of God is not coming in ways that can be observed, nor will they say, 'Look, here it is!' or 'There!' for behold, the kingdom of God is in the midst of you."*
> *- Luke 17:20-21*

It is not coming in ways that can be observed. It's not a thing you can see or point to on a map. It is somehow connected to the people, both of his day and of ours. This is the most important point for our discussion: the kingdom of God is not physical. *It cannot be physical*:

> *I tell you this, brothers: flesh and blood cannot inherit the kingdom of God, nor does the perishable inherit the imperishable.*
> — 1 Corinthians 15:50

Jesus's kingdom is not bound by the physical things of creation: time, space, distance, matter, and geography. When questioned by Pilate, who thought in these mundane terms, this is what he had to say:

> *So Pilate entered his headquarters again and called Jesus and said to him, "Are you the King of the Jews?" Jesus answered, "Do you say this of your own accord, or did others say it to you about me?" Pilate answered, "Am I a Jew? Your own nation and the chief priests have delivered you over to me. What have you done?" Jesus answered, "My kingdom is not of this world. If my kingdom were of this world, my servants would have been fighting, that I might not be delivered over to the Jews. But my kingdom is not from the world." Then Pilate said to him, "So you are a king?" Jesus answered, "You say that I am a king. For this purpose I was born and for this purpose I have come into the world—to bear witness to the truth. Everyone who is of the truth listens to my voice."*
> — John 18:33-37

Pilate was concerned with a very earthly thing: Was Jesus claiming to be the physical ruler of the people that he (Pilate) was supposed to be governing? Pilate's motives were easy to understand. Was he going to have to quell a rebellion or fight a war? But Jesus says that Pilate isn't thinking the right way: "*My kingdom is not of this world.*"

We must not create a false equivalence between America

(or any other earthly nation or kingdom) and God's nation. To be clear, no earthly nation is "God's nation." The Kingdom (or Realm or Nation or Country) that Christ established is not such a paltry, ordinary thing (Revelation 7:9-12)!

There is a passage in 1 Peter (a book we will focus on for a bit) that comes close to using the phrase "Christian nation":

> *But you are a chosen race, a royal priesthood, a holy nation, a people for his own possession, that you may proclaim the excellencies of him who called you out of darkness into his marvelous light. Once you were not a people, but now you are God's people; once you had not received mercy, but now you have received mercy.*
> - 1 Peter 2:9-10

Who was Peter writing to? It wasn't 21st century Americans, right? He was writing to the "elect exiles of the Dispersion" (1 Peter 1:1), those Christian Jews scattered throughout several regions of the Mediterranean world. *They* were the holy nation. By extension, every Christian who reads 1 Peter can be included in that holy nation. Think about what that means! God's nation is not something that has existed on a single continent for the last 200 years; God's nation exists across time and geography, in any part of the world that has Christians. If we ever colonize Mars, and Christians go there, then that will also be part of God's nation! If America were to implode tomorrow, God's kingdom would not be diminished, because God's nation is not dependent on America or its government. The Christians who live on the land that used to be America would not suddenly be excluded from God's nation just because the government collapsed. To limit the nation of God to one country is the opposite of glorifying God: it is limiting, it is shrinking, it is diminishing what Christ established! How dare we do such a thing!

We keep reading in 1 Peter:

> *Beloved, I urge you as sojourners and exiles to abstain from the passions of the flesh, which wage war against your soul. Keep your conduct among the Gentiles honorable, so that when they speak against you as evildoers, they may see your good deeds and glorify God on the day of visitation.*
> - *1 Peter 2:11-12*

If we think of ourselves as Americans first, who are also Christians, then we have not adopted the mindset of Jesus or the early Church. There was an interesting double meaning in this passage for the original audience; they were members of an earthly kingdom (Israel), who had been exiled to different earthly kingdoms. However, that was not their true exile. Their sojourning was not primarily as Jews in the Roman Empire; their travels were that of a heavenly citizen through the nations of earth!

To be sure, I don't think many who long to return to a "Christian nation" would claim to be "American first, Christian second," but the problem is that we often act as if it were true, regardless of what we would claim. We talk about America more than we talk about Christianity. We evangelize America more than we evangelize the gospel (trying to convince people of the goodness of America more than trying to convince people of the goodness of God). We get more upset about people hurting America than people hurting the Church (the temple of God, remember!). We spend more time watching and listening to political shows than we do studying God's word. We confuse patriotic ethics with Christian ethics. We allow the government to dictate morality, instead of scripture. When we do these things, regardless of what we want to portray to the world, it will seem as if we care more about our earthly country than our heavenly one. It will seem so because, for all practical purposes, it is so.

We are Christians who coincidentally live in America (or China or Africa or any other place). Our duty to God would not be substantially different if we were in another country. Our journey through this life, in this nation, is merely a proving ground on an eternal journey toward heaven. We are strangers or exiles here, like the people commended in Hebrews 11 for having the greatest faith:

> *These all died in faith, not having received the things promised, but having seen them and greeted them from afar, and having acknowledged that they were strangers and exiles on the earth. For people who speak thus make it clear that they are seeking a homeland. If they had been thinking of that land from which they had gone out, they would have had opportunity to return. But as it is, they desire a better country, that is, a heavenly one. Therefore God is not ashamed to be called their God, for he has prepared for them a city.*
>
> *- Hebrews 11:13-16*

The city that God has prepared is not New York City, Shanghai, or London. *It is a heavenly one.* That is to say, it is something that doesn't exist in one location on earth. So, this is the first step to properly glorifying God in America: we must think of this country, however great we consider it to be, as a mission field. It is a place we travel to with the express purpose of teaching and reaching the lost, but it is not itself the Kingdom. No matter how nice it is or how pleasant it is to live in, it cannot compare to the glory that waits.

The part of our identity that says we are American is, at best, the eighth-most important thing about us. In a generally

Biblical order, we might rank them: child of God, Christian brother or sister, light of the world, gender (which has a lot of application in Scripture), spouse (if applicable), parent (if applicable), child, friend, and then maybe (MAYBE!), American. But really, we could lump all the physical markers of identity in the same group (race, nationality, ethnicity, etc.), as the least important part of our identity.

BUT, WE STILL LIVE HERE

Of course, there are still important things we need to consider about glorifying God in our earthly country, because this is the particular circumstance in which we find ourselves. This is the place we can influence the lost for Christ. The Christian is not completely separate from their nation, and we are told in Scripture that we *do* have some obligation toward the country in which we happen to live. What is expected of the Christian in this regard? What sorts of things should we consider in our specific earthly context? Peter, in the next few verses, has some insight:

> *Be subject for the Lord's sake to every human institution, whether it be to the emperor as supreme, or to governors as sent by him to punish those who do evil and to praise those who do good. For this is the will of God, that by doing good you should put to silence the ignorance of foolish people. Live as people who are free, not using your freedom as a cover-up for evil, but living as servants of God. Honor everyone. Love the brotherhood. Fear God. Honor the emperor.*
> *- 1 Peter 2:13-17*

This might be a difficult question for some: did you honor Barack Obama? He was, for a time, the modern equivalent of our emperor. What about the Senate or the governor or the members of the House of Representatives? What about Trump? What about Biden, now? Peter probably wrote this letter either during the reign of Nero or Domitian. Nero was a tyrant who persecuted Christians mercilessly and caused great devastation to Rome. Domitian viewed himself as an enlightened agent of Jupiter (the chief Roman deity) and worked hard to impose the traditional Roman religion on everyone. Yet, Peter says to "honor the emperor"! Jesus said a very similar thing when he told people to "render to Caesar the things that are Caesar's" (Luke 20:22-26). Why? How could Jesus and Peter have this attitude?

This is part of the command we have already read in v. 12: "Keep your conduct among the Gentiles honorable, so that when they speak against you as evildoers, they may see your good deeds and glorify God on the day of visitation." Part of the practical way Peter wanted them to carry out this command, in order that God would be glorified, was to be subject to the earthly government they lived under, even though the rulers were blatantly anti-God! He did not command them to rise up or try to change policy or campaign against the evil dictator.

This is not a command we can switch on or off, based on how closely the current regime aligns with our personal morals! This is not an optional extra of Christianity; this is a direct command, and it is a command repeated multiple times in the New Testament:

> *Remind them to be submissive to rulers and authorities, to be obedient, to be ready for every good work, to speak evil of no one, to avoid quarreling, to be gentle, and to show perfect courtesy toward all people.*
> *- Titus 3:1-2*

What exactly are we commanded to do in this passage? The way these commands can specifically be applied to our modern context can only be providential (almost as if the Spirit who inspired the words knew that they would be needed for Christians of all eras):

1. To speak evil of no one. How many of our Facebook, Twitter, or Instagram posts speak badly of those who have a different political view than ourselves? What about our conversations with friends and family? Do we disparage those in power who do things we don't like? Do we mock our coworkers who advocate for different policies than we prefer?

2. To avoid quarreling. Is there anything we quarrel about more than politics? Do we even try to avoid it? Has such quarreling ever resulted in harmonious relationships and unified thoughts?

3. To be gentle. This is the same word used in Philippians 4:5: "let your *reasonableness* be known to everyone." Would someone discussing politics with you describe you as "reasonable" or "gentle"? Remember, there is a difference between having a disagreement and being disparaging. God doesn't expect us to agree with everyone, but He does expect us to be gentle in our disagreement.

4. To show perfect courtesy toward all people. Note the express command not to do the "bare minimum." Don't show a "decent amount" of courtesy, or a "passing courtesy." Show *perfect* courtesy. Do we have to do this even to those who don't share our political beliefs? Wouldn't those people be part of the group "all people"?

What happens when we don't demonstrate these attitudes? This is when we start to present a false glory and dishonor God in this area of life. If we allow our care for political matters to override God's commands about how to treat people, then we demonstrate our true priorities. It dishonors

God when His children choose the satisfaction of anger, harsh words, and conflict over the pursuit of peace, edification, and evangelism.

It's not wrong to care about the country in which we live, unless we allow that care to rule over our behavior. Caring about our country becomes wrong when it clouds the purpose God has given us to glorify Him and reach the lost above all. Mistreating the lost person that disagrees with your politics results in God being diminished in their eyes!

When we put political or national issues on the same level as spiritual ones, we present the world with a false glory! If your first instinct is "How can I convince this person to agree with my politics?" and not "How can I convince this person of the Truth of the Gospel?" then your priorities are wrong.

After reminding Titus why all this mattered and what kind of heathens the Christians used to be before the grace of God, this is how Paul ended this section of the letter to Titus:

> *The saying is trustworthy, and I want you to insist on these things, so that those who have believed in God may be careful to devote themselves to good works. These things are excellent and profitable for people. But avoid foolish controversies, genealogies, dissensions, and quarrels about the law, for they are unprofitable and worthless.*
>
> - Titus 3:8-9

If I may, allow this book to be part of my fulfilling of Paul's command to the preacher (the role Titus had and the role I have): I *insist* that you demonstrate these qualities in your engagement with politics and your country. I do not ask; I do not suggest; I *insist*.

(As a side note, based on the context, it is very possible that Paul's use of the word "law" here is referring to civil law!

Submit to rulers and authorities...and do not quarrel about the law!)

Does this mean that we need to agree with everything the government does? Of course not! Peter and Paul would not have agreed with Nero if and when he tried to blame the fire of Rome on Christians. However, we also have no record whatsoever that they tried to publicly denounce him or protest against his policies, and we don't know how they discussed it privately.

As we read these texts, an important question emerges: What political activity do we see in the lives of the apostles in the New Testament? What about in the life of Jesus? Did they make any effort to change anything about the human government they lived under? If they had wanted to, could they have enacted change throughout the empire? They could strike people blind with a word and raise an army from the dead – no force could have stood against them! If they had wanted to remake Rome in the image of Israel, they certainly could have done it! So, why didn't they?

The apostles had more ability to affect worldly political change than any other members of Jesus's new kingdom that have ever lived or who ever will live. If they made precisely zero attempt to do so, what can or should we infer from that for our own application? What does it say about the Spirit's priorities that He did not inspire them to enact political change? If He had wanted a physical nation reborn in the image of Israel, why wouldn't He have had the apostles take Rome?

Why Does This Matter?

First of all, then, I urge that supplications, prayers, intercessions, and thanksgivings be made for all people,

for kings and all who are in high positions, that we may lead a peaceful and quiet life, godly and dignified in every way.
- 1 Timothy 2:1-2

We *are* told to attempt to change the government in one specific way: through prayer. But note what that means: We aren't the ones doing the changing – God is! We are asking God to do it instead of taking it into our own hands. What should we desire? To lead a peaceful and quiet life. What we should care about is our ability to live righteously. We may hate the sin in the lives of the lost and despair over how the world tramples God, but our ability to be a Christian has not been significantly hampered in this country, despite what we see in the news. If you live in America, you almost certainly met to worship this week without molestation and you can talk to your neighbors and friends about Christ almost without repercussion. We have so far to go before things are even close to as bad as they were at the time all these commands were written (though, in some parts of the world, Christians *do* face challenges that are hard to imagine). Again, why are we commanded this?

...it is pleasing in the sight of God our Savior, who desires all people to be saved and to come to the knowledge of the truth.
- 1 Timothy 2:3-4

But you are a chosen race, a royal priesthood, a holy nation, a people for his own possession, that you may proclaim the excellencies of him who called you out of darkness into his marvelous light.
- 1 Peter 2:9

> *Keep your conduct among the Gentiles honorable, so that when they speak against you as evildoers, they may see your good deeds and glorify God on the day of visitation.*
>
> — 1 Peter 2:12

The point of our brief sojourn in exile on this planet is not to remake our government into God's image: that is impossible! It's to influence as many people as we can for the sake of the gospel! Individual change, not national, is the mandate of the Christian. The fact that the apostles, divinely inspired and empowered, made no attempts to enforce Christianity on a national level implies that they thought that soul-reaching is best accomplished locally and outside the political arena! If the Spirit thought they could be more effective in proclaiming the Gospel of Christ by enacting Christian legislation, don't you think He would have told them to do so?

More to the point, think about the people in your life who are the most politically active, especially those who have different politics than you do. Are you more likely to engage with them because they are overtly adamant about their politics? Why would you think the opposite would suddenly be true when you do it? The goal is not to convince people that capitalism is better than socialism or the other way around; the point is to convince people that they are lost and in need of the blood of Christ! What does the economy have to do with that? Even a matter like abortion, that does have spiritual significance, should not be primarily engaged on a political level. Only by turning people to Christ do we have a hope of convincing them of the truth in any specific area.

Turning America into a modern version of ancient Israel, a theocracy with God at the head, is not the thing that would be most glorifying to God. It's not something that God commanded us to do. It's not even an accomplishable goal. The apostles and prophets had to spend decades convincing people that God doesn't relate to people through one specific, earthly nation anymore. This is the core conflict of the book of Acts, as the Jews had a very hard time adjusting to the fact that God viewed their nation as equal with all the other nations after the ascension of Christ. God's covenant through Christ is not mediated through a particular country, and many Israelites refused to accept that fact.

Yet, I fear many people want to go back to that First Covenant model with America in the place of ancient Israel as the instrument of God's will on the earth. Every time this has happened in the last two thousand years (for example, Constantinople or the Crusades) it has ended disastrously, with wholesale corruption of the Word of God. The Church must be independent from the needs and demands of any specific nation; that is the only way it can truly be a unifying force for all of humanity.

Convincing your neighbor of Jesus' love and convicting your coworker that they need forgiveness from God; those are things that will glorify our Savior. Incidentally, if we change enough individuals and inspire enough discipleship, the country will end up with laws that are more in line with Christianity, because that's how laws form in this country, by the will of the people. It will never (and should never) be the other way around. That is precisely why there was a time when the culture and legislation of the country seemed to line up more with Biblical truth. During that time, more people generally believed in God and the Bible. If you want that to be the case again, get out and evangelize!

And really, when you think about it, don't you want to live in a country where the laws are formed by the will of the people? You can't suddenly start disliking the model because you are now in the minority. If you think this is the best model of governance, that shouldn't change when the will of the people changes. Remember, Jesus taught that Christians would normally be in the minority (Matthew 7:13-14)!

WHAT ABOUT LAWS THAT CONTRADICT THE BIBLE?

Yes, there are laws that are clearly evil. There always have been. We needn't endorse every policy that comes from our government. Did Peter approved of Domitian's policy that everyone should worship Jupiter in addition to whatever other gods they worshipped? It would be dishonoring to God to act as if we believed untrue or wicked things were true and good. Consider, however, the *scale* of such disagreements in the New Testament and the scope of Christian dissent against the government. It was always on the local level, first engaging friends and family, and always under the umbrella of submission to the rulers with humility. There were times when Christians were forced to choose death and prison instead of submission to laws that would force them to violate God's commands, but there is not a single law in America that would force me to make that choice. Maybe that time will come; but even if it does, consider some more words of Peter:

> *Beloved, do not be surprised at the fiery trial when it comes upon you to test you, as though something strange were happening to you. But rejoice insofar as you share Christ's sufferings, that you may also rejoice and be glad when his glory is revealed. If you are insulted for the name of Christ, you are blessed, because the Spirit of glory and of God rests upon you.*
> *- 1 Peter 4:12-14*

But America Started out Christian

If you long for a return to a time when most Americans were Christians, consider that there has never been such a time. There have been times when most people believed in God (still true for now) and times when most people held the Bible in high regard (not true anymore), but there has never been a time when the majority of Americans believed in adult immersion for forgiveness of sins or submitted to the Biblical structure of Church leadership or emulated the early Christians in worship practices. If the founding fathers (many of whom were "Christians" only in the broadest sense of the word) were suddenly alive today, I suspect many would not feel comfortable fellowshipping or worshipping with them. They did not teach the whole truth about salvation or worship, even if they did believe in God and the importance of Scripture. It would be easier, in some ways, if more people generally believed in the Bible as they once did; but remember that even at the peak of Christianity in American history, there were not substantially more people who taught immersion for the forgiveness of sins or worshipped according to the example of the New Testament Church. So, as Solomon said:

> *Say not, "Why were the former days better than these?" For it is not from wisdom that you ask this.*
> *- Ecclesiastes 7:10*

Trying to Stay Positive

Finally, let us end with some positive words. I know that many are struggling, depressed over the "way things are going." It can be demoralizing, but change is possible! It's not going to happen through legislation, but it can happen nonetheless! How can it happen?

1. The primary method we have of changing the world is by teaching the lost. It's not surprising when people who don't know God live contrary to Him. Our job is to teach the truth to all people. Most will probably not respond, but some surely will! God is able to provide growth for His people who are diligently doing His will! The people we are most likely to affect positively with our teaching are the people in our neighborhoods, offices, and families, not the people in another state or city. There are people in your life that need to be taught, and we have an obligation and privilege to do so!

2. The best way we can stand out as "lights in the world" is by living differently. Our lives should look and be different than the majority around us. We should treat people better, have better relationships, and prioritize different things. The darkness of the world provides great contrast for the brightness of God's people, and we should capitalize on that! Read through the passages in 1 Peter again: what are we to do? "Keep our conduct...honorable," "abstain from the passions of the flesh," "proclaim His excellencies," and "live as servants of God." "By doing good you should put to silence the ignorance of foolish people." We have great opportunity in America to do these things, without fear of death or imprisonment that many in the world face for such behavior. Do we take advantage of this great gift?

3. The ebb and flow of nations is not new or unique to our time. There are many different fields ready for spiritual harvest, and no two are exactly alike. Culture swings toward and away from God on a pretty regular basis. Perhaps we are living in a time of difficulty, but we know that God is still in control and knows best how to balance what His people need.

If we live out these principles, the culture can absolutely start looking more and more like a place influenced by God.

Even if we can't affect the country, we can certainly impact the place we live. Change is possible, but only if we realize the true mission of the Christian and the church. We are here for a little while, and whether we are in America or China or Zimbabwe, our goal is the same: to be the "pillar and buttress of the truth" (1 Timothy 3:15), especially to the people in our lives!

DIGGING DEEPER

1. Why do so many people (maybe even you) invest so much of their identity and effort into the nation in which they live? What spiritual problems does prioritizing our nation lead to?

2. In what ways did the first century church struggle with the tension between national and spiritual identity? How does our struggle mirror theirs? How is our different?

3. Do you know of any places today where Christians regularly have to risk being arrested in order to live godly lives? What can you do to support them or give them strength?

4. If someone who doesn't know you were to have access to a schedule of how you normally spend your time or a list of the things you normally post on social media, would they think you care more about politics or spirituality?

10. *Digital Glory: A New World*

Jesus commanded his disciples to "go into all the world and proclaim the gospel to the whole creation" (Mark 16:15). Paul said that he would "become all things to all people, that by all means I might save some" (1 Corinthians 9:22). Both of these scriptures should inform how we engage with the internet. As more and more people spend larger portions of their time online, the digital world that people inhabit becomes the place we must go to reach them. If we are going to adopt Paul's philosophy of doing "all to the glory of God" (1 Corinthians 10:31), we must figure out how to be online in a way that glorifies God and reaches the lost.

Because there are many struggles and difficulties that we must grapple with online, we might feel tempted to forgo the internet altogether, but it is reasonable to conclude that this is not what Jesus and Paul would have done. The command to go into all the world and the example of becoming all things to all people means that we need to learn how to use the internet well, rather than avoiding it altogether.

There are two ways to think about the internet. The first is the reasoning that because there are bad things on the internet, the whole internet is bad. But even if this were the correct way to think, we might consider Paul going to Mars Hill in Acts 17, a place full of pagan idol worship. Did the idolatry keep Paul from attempting to reach the people there?

In reality, though, just because there is bad stuff on the internet doesn't mean that the internet is inherently bad. That would be like saying that because there is crime in America, all of America is bad. The internet is full of good, bad, and morally neutral content and sites, but the internet itself is morally neutral. It's just a place.

So, what are some of the primary pitfalls of internet use for the Christian, as well as some ways we can use it to exalt our Lord?

Glory Begins in the Heart and Mind

Way back at the beginning of this book, we started with the idea that before we can glorify God in our actions and words, we must glorify God in our thoughts and emotions. God's exaltation happens on an individual level before it can ever happen on a public or corporate level. This is just as true online as it is in person.

The primary thing the internet has done for people is give them access to vast amounts of information and media. In the United States there are almost zero controls over who can access what. Many countries restrict access to certain content on a national level, meaning that the internet service providers themselves have to block some websites from reaching the individual user's network, or the country itself blocks the content from reaching the local servers in the first place. The Unite States does not currently do this. This means we have access to a great treasure of knowledge and inspiration, but it also means we have access to a quagmire of corrupting and degrading content.

Unfortunately, humanity has always faced the problem of corrupting influences, so this is not particularly new. What has dramatically increased is the variety of information available and the speed and ease with which we can consume it. As technology continues to improve, so, too, do Satan's tempting schemes.

> *Finally, brothers, whatever is true, whatever is honorable, whatever is just, whatever is pure, whatever is lovely, whatever is commendable, if there is any excellence, if there is anything worthy of praise, think about these things.*
> *- Philippians 4:8*

Spend some time and effort to memorize this verse! Are there honorable, just, pure, lovely, commendable, and excellent things on the internet? Of course there are! This is one of the primary benefits of the internet. I can view inspiring, praiseworthy content from across the globe! If I want to develop the habit of glorifying God, this is the kind of content I should seek out.

> *For where your treasure is, there your heart will be also.*
>
> *"The eye is the lamp of the body. So, if your eye is healthy, your whole body will be full of light, but if your eye is bad, your whole body will be full of darkness. If then the light in you is darkness, how great is the darkness!*
> *- Matthew 6:21-23*

This text highlights why it is so important that we learn to use the internet in a God-glorifying way. We must consider what we allow into our souls through what we see and experience.

It is easy to get sucked down the rabbit hole of negative,

alarmist, or detrimental content on the internet. Once we start down that path it can very easily become addictive, just like negative behavior and emotions can become addictive in real life! The brain can get trapped in a pleasure-inducing dopamine loop of sensationalist or sinful internet content as much as it can trashy TV or harmful gossip with your friends.

It's not wrong to spend time on the internet. It *is* wrong to let the internet drag us into thinking about and dwelling on things that are neither beneficial nor glorifying to our Creator.

THE ALLURE OF ANONYMITY

One of the key aspects of glory is *reputation*. Glorifying God is, in many ways, the betterment and increase of God's reputation among people. To dishonor God is to worsen His reputation!

We have looked at the following verses numerous times in this book because they are so apt, but, as you read them this time, consider how they might apply to the internet:

> *You are the light of the world. A city set on a hill cannot be hidden. Nor do people light a lamp and put it under a basket, but on a stand, and it gives light to all in the house. In the same way, let your light shine before others, so that they may see your good works and give glory to your Father who is in heaven.*
>
> *- Matthew 5:14-16*

We are supposed to be the light and the city that people see, representing God to the world. Note what Jesus says about hiding that light or city: "a city...cannot be hidden. Nor do people light a lamp and put it under a basket...." In order to be the light of the world, people need to know who we are and that we claim to represent Christ.

If no one knows you are a Christian, the content you post can't possibly increase the reputation of the God you serve. Therefore, anonymous internet posting can potentially inhibit your effort to glorify God.

Additionally, the allure of anonymity – of no one knowing who you are – carries with it an insidious temptation...

> *For everyone who does wicked things hates the light and does not come to the light, lest his works should be exposed. But whoever does what is true comes to the light, so that it may be clearly seen that his works have been carried out in God.*
>
> *- John 3:20-21*

This is a classic chicken-egg situation. Do people seek anonymity so that they can act unrighteously, or do people act unrighteously because they happen to be posting anonymously? Like many such dualities, it's probably both in most circumstances. They feed off each other. When no one knows who I am, I can behave wickedly without having to physically or immediately face the consequences of my actions. We might think that because no one knows who we are, we can't damage our reputation or the reputation of the Church or God by indulging our desire to be hateful, angry, or ungracious.

Maybe, for a time, this might be true. But on the internet, nothing is ever gone. How many times have you seen a public figure get into trouble for something they said or did months or years or decades ago? The allure of anonymity, like many other sins, is a "fleeting pleasure" (Hebrews 11:25).

I'm not trying to suggest that we have to put our personal identifying information on everything we do online, but especially on social media, if your goal is to glorify God what purpose does anonymity serve? If your goal is to elevate God and increase the reputation of His Church, how does online anonymity help you accomplish that?

We must take special care not to fall into the snares of the Devil in this way and fall prey to the allure of anonymity!

> *Take no part in the unfruitful works of darkness, but instead expose them. For it is shameful even to speak of the things that they do in secret. But when anything is exposed by the light, it becomes visible, for anything that becomes visible is light. Therefore it says, "Awake, O sleeper, and arise from the dead, and Christ will shine on you." Look carefully then how you walk, not as unwise but as wise, making the best use of the time, because the days are evil.*
>
> *- Ephesians 5:11-16*

THE OPPOSITE OF GLORY

By far, the biggest online detriment to the glory of God is Christians who live one way in real life and a totally different way online. There is a word for such behavior: hypocrisy. When we do this, we become like Peter at one of his low points:

> *But when Cephas came to Antioch, I opposed him to his face, because he stood condemned. For before certain men came from James, he was eating with the Gentiles; but when they came he drew back and separated himself, fearing the circumcision party. And the rest of the Jews acted hypocritically along with him, so that even Barnabas was led astray by their hypocrisy.*
>
> *- Galatians 2:11-13*

In Peter's case, the hypocrisy was behaving one way

around the Gentiles and another way around the Jews. Paul's point was clear: If Peter knew something was right or true, he needed to act as if it was so, no matter who was around him! The same principle is just as important when we consider our online activity. We mustn't claim to live righteously or be righteous people while we continually act like trashy, horrible people online.

In this vein, all the scriptures that talk about our words apply to words that are typed in addition to words that are spoken:

> *Let no corrupting talk come out of your mouths, but only such as is good for building up, as fits the occasion, that it may give grace to those who hear.*
> *- Ephesians 4:29*

> *Walk in wisdom toward outsiders, making the best use of the time. Let your speech always be gracious, seasoned with salt, so that you may know how you ought to answer each person.*
> *- Colossians 4:5-6*

It is dangerously easy to post something online that tears down rather than builds up. Online, we don't have to see the face of the person we are destroying or face the immediate fallout for our careless words. It's easy to push any guilt from our minds when there aren't tangible consequences. It's hard to "give grace to those who hear" when we don't see the hearer.

But these commands apply to our posts and statuses and tweets as much as they do to our conversations!

> *I tell you, on the day of judgment people will give account for every careless word they speak, for by your*

words you will be justified, and by your words you will be condemned.
- Matthew 12:36-37

How many "careless words" have we put out into the world via our keyboards? Do you think God is keeping a record of those words as well? Why would we think that suddenly God doesn't care just because there aren't soundwaves involved? And while these things ultimately affect our own eternal judgment, there is broader harm that online hypocrisy causes:

You who boast in the law dishonor God by breaking the law. For, as it is written, "The name of God is blasphemed among the Gentiles because of you."
- Romans 2:23-24

The lost are not stupid! They are online like we are, and they see what we say, what we do, and how we act. And, if we are not hiding behind the veil of anonymity, they see our claim of Christianity, and they will blaspheme the name of God "because of you [us]." This is the exact opposite of glorifying God! If someone thinks less of God or His people (the Church) because of our online behavior, then we have diminished God. We have failed in the most awful way!

If your right eye causes you to sin, tear it out and throw it away. For it is better that you lose one of your members than that your whole body be thrown into hell. And if your right hand causes you to sin, cut it off and throw it away. For it is better that you lose one of your members than that your whole body go into hell.
- Matthew 5:29-30

For some of us, the benefits of using the internet might not be worth the potential dishonor our misuse will bring to God

If internet use is consistently causing you to sin, perhaps you need to take a break and step back from it. Maybe some of us need to take some time developing self-control before we enter back into the temptations that the internet presents.

> ...but no human being can tame the tongue. It is a restless evil, full of deadly poison. With it we bless our Lord and Father, and with it we curse people who are made in the likeness of God. From the same mouth come blessing and cursing. My brothers, these things ought not to be so. Does a spring pour forth from the same opening both fresh and salt water? Can a fig tree, my brothers, bear olives, or a grapevine produce figs? Neither can a salt pond yield fresh water. Who is wise and understanding among you? By his good conduct let him show his works in the meekness of wisdom. But if you have bitter jealousy and selfish ambition in your hearts, do not boast and be false to the truth.
> - James 3:8-14

Our words online must be held to the same standard as words in person. We "ought not" say edifying, uplifting, blessing words in real life and then hateful, cursing, thoughtless words online. The requirements for righteousness aren't any less important on the internet.

We all have to ask ourselves, "why do I use this particular online platform?" (be it Facebook or Twitter or Pinterest or anything else). If my primary reason for being online is to gain a following or promote myself, then I am probably not living for God's glory. I am probably demonstrating "selfish ambition." If my primary reason for using the internet is to satisfy "the desires of the flesh," then my behavior is not contributing to God's glory!

There are many positive reasons for being on the internet: contact with friends, inspiration from good sources, keeping up with world events, and being a good influence on others. However, there are just as many (if not more) negative reasons for internet use. As in all matters, wise and discerning internet use begins with "the meekness of wisdom."

THE KEY TO GLORY

> *Do you not know that in a race all the runners run, but only one receives the prize? So run that you may obtain it. Every athlete exercises self-control in all things. They do it to receive a perishable wreath, but we an imperishable. So I do not run aimlessly; I do not box as one beating the air.*
> - 1 Corinthians 9:24-26

Really, this whole discussion comes down to one of the fundamental Christian traits: self-control. Several of the normal external forces that aid us in self-control are absent online, and there are even more factors that encourage forsaking self-control on the internet. We don't have to see the faces of the people we are insulting, feel the weight of peer pressure to use manners, or prepare for the immediate consequence that our words would bring in person. Inflammatory content tends to get more likes and shares, and so we are slowly trained by the endorphin rush to post more and more derogatory or controversial content. No one sees us consuming the content that poisons our hearts and minds, so we don't feel quite so guilty about it.

None of this is an excuse not to use the internet; they are simply reasons to be vigilant! The internet can be a great tool for righteousness and God's glory, if we can maintain control of ourselves! So, if we want to take advantage of the great opportunity afforded to us by the internet, what should we do?

10 WAYS TO GLORIFY GOD ON THE INTERNET

1. Before you post something, read it out loud. I think we might be surprised how something can sound benign in our heads, but when it is said out loud, it sounds horrible.

2. Ask yourself, "what's the worst possible way this could be taken?" Many people will interpret anything on the internet in the worst possible way. Obviously, you can't control other people, but you can do everything in your power to phrase things exactly the way you want them to be understood.

3. Consider how you would feel if someone said to you what you are saying online. This is just the golden rule (Matthew 7:12).

4. Don't post anything online you wouldn't be willing to say in person. This is especially true on public forums like Facebook or Twitter. Don't let the allure of physical separation remove your control of your tongue.

5. Memorize Philippians 4:8. Does what you are about to post or share fall into one or more of the categories Paul lists? If not, why not? Is it something that other people should be thinking about? If not, then why are you presenting it to them?

6. Stop airing your grievances with other people online!

> *So if you have such cases, why do you lay them before those who have no standing in the church? I say this to your shame. Can it be that there is no one among you wise enough to settle a dispute between the*

> *brothers, but brother goes to law against brother, and that before unbelievers? To have lawsuits at all with one another is already a defeat for you. Why not rather suffer wrong? Why not rather be defrauded?*
> - 1 Corinthians 6:4-7

Setting aside the fact that working out our conflicts in public is simply wrong, consider how such behavior affects God's reputation and the Church's reputation in the community. Why would someone want to be a part of a church community that is always fighting? Maybe we aren't always fighting, but if someone only knows us from our online presence, is that what they see of us?

Also, we may think that we are being so subtle, passive aggressively posting something like "I can't believe some people! You know who you are!" We aren't fooling anyone. All it does is make us look immature and petty.

7. Follow, share, and subscribe to things that glorify God. The internet can be a vicious, merciless place. People make money based on what sites and pages are viewed and shared, and if something doesn't get viewed, it gets abandoned or cut. Web hosting isn't free. If you want honorable, pure, truthful, praiseworthy content to thrive on the internet, following and sharing can go a long way to making sure the creators of that content can continue to do so.

8. Pray for wisdom.

> *If any of you lacks wisdom, let him ask God, who gives generously to all without reproach, and it will be given him. - James 1:5*

9. Learn how to send direct messages on every platform you use. While conflict is almost always better solved in person, there are times when you might need to say something that would be a stumbling block to someone viewing a public post without all the context. There are myriad contexts when sending a private message is better than posting on the public part of the website. Learn how to do that on each site you use.

10. Don't post in the heat of the moment. This is good advice for real-life confrontations, not just for internet use. If you are particularly emotional, take some time to level out before you post online.

Digging Deeper

1. Do you spend a lot of time on the internet or social media? Why might it be important even for people who don't to know the things in this chapter?

2. Have you ever seen a passive aggressive post and instantly knew what it was about, even though it didn't mention anything specific? What does this imply about your own passive-aggressiveness?

3. List some good ways you could use the internet or good sites to visit. How often do you use the internet that way or promote or post about those things or sites? Why is that?

4. When was the last time you "unplugged" and took a break from social media (Facebook, Instagram, Twitter, etc.)? Try to spend a week without using those sites (outside work needs) and do so *without posting about your social media fast*. After, consider how difficult it was or how it made you feel.

11. Financial Glory: The Power and Danger of Choice

As an integral, central part of life, money can be an avenue for great glory or great dishonor. How can we use money to elevate and glorify God?

Most of this chapter will revolve around the concept of *discretionary spending,* or the ability to buy things above and beyond what we need. This is the primary way the Bible talks about wealth and richness.

Paul gives us a pretty good definition of "need":

> But godliness with contentment is great gain, for we brought nothing into the world, and we cannot take anything out of the world. But if we have food and clothing, with these we will be content. But those who desire to be rich fall into temptation, into a snare, into many senseless and harmful desires that plunge people into ruin and destruction.
> - 1 Timothy 6:6-9

The contrast between "the desire to be rich" and "with these we will be content" is important. The United States, perhaps more than any other country in history, is focused on excess and luxury, on accruing wealth beyond the necessity.

Is it wrong to have more than what we need? No, for reasons we will discuss later. However, it is wrong to be discontented. The *desire* to be rich is the temptation (or snare).

Consider the amount of your budget that is dedicated toward unnecessary experiences or things (necessary things would be food, clothing, etc.). This is the "discretionary" part of your budget because it involves choice. It is at your discretion. God understands that the necessities are not really a choice because we need them to survive, but so much of what we buy (in this country especially) is not a need. It is a choice afforded to us (pun intended) by excess.

Our choices demonstrate our priorities and show the world what we care about. This is true in our self-declared politics and sexual identities, in the way we dress, and in the things we buy. With greater flexibility of choice comes greater responsibility to choose wisely. In our country we not only have many options of what to buy, but also where to buy it! Our choices will either glorify or dishonor God.

There are some tricky, messy topics in the area of personal finance, topics that I am not entirely settled on myself. I hope that as we discuss these things we will all consider how to elevate, praise, and honor our Creator and Savior.

Money Creates Options

This is the true power of wealth: the ability to be selective about what we buy and where. The average person in America might be able to buy a car, but only the super-wealthy have the option to buy any car in the world. The less money you have, the more restricted you are in what kind of car you can buy. More money creates more options. These options, or lack thereof, play an important role in our glorifying of God. What should the priority of our wealth be?

> *Command these things as well, so that they may be without reproach. But if anyone does not provide for his relatives, and especially for members of his household, he has denied the faith and is worse than an unbeliever.*
> - 1 Timothy 5:7-8

This passage comes right before Paul's statement about being content with food and clothing. Not just in finances, but in all areas of life, one of the primary ways we glorify God is by obeying His will. God has shown us His will in regard to finances: He wants us to provide for our families!

Perhaps some people worry that because they can't afford to give more to God, they are violating His commands or are not good enough for Him. God is not unclear: Provide for your family! There is an important caveat, however:

> *For even when we were with you, we would give you this command: If anyone is not willing to work, let him not eat. For we hear that some among you walk in idleness, not busy at work, but busybodies. Now such persons we command and encourage in the Lord Jesus Christ to do their work quietly and to earn their own living.*
> - 2 Thessalonians 3:10-12

God understands the basic priority of human needs because He made us and understands all things. More than that, He understands our hearts and intents. If we are working the best we can, God understands that! Of course, God will hold us accountable if we are lazy and overly reliant on others.

More money creates more options. For those with less money, those options become more restricted. For some people, the answer to the question "How do I glorify God with money?" is answered simply by providing for your family and giving to the Lord on the first day of the week. You may not have the funds to do more than that; to do otherwise is to become "worse than an unbeliever"! Think about it from the perspective of reputation; glory is a matter of reputation. How does it reflect on God if we won't prioritize our families? Even the world does that!

NEED CREATES OPPORTUNITIES

Of course, we understand that even working our hardest sometimes isn't good enough. Let me be clear: there are times when a person's financial struggles are not their fault! Having the attitude "well, just get a better job," is not only incredibly condescending, it is unhelpful, uncaring, and quite possibly sinful. Are there people who are only in need because of laziness and poor choices? Sure! However, there are many more who are in need because we live in a fallen world, and society is full of imperfect people and oppression. Sometimes it is possible to improve your life standing, and sometimes it isn't. Sometimes people have genuine need, and they can't just "make better choices" to acquire what is needed. Some people do not have the talent or ability to make an abundance of money.

But with need comes opportunity for glory. For those of us who have abundance, there is one monetary habit that glorifies God more than any other: generosity!

> *As for the rich in this present age, charge them not to be haughty, nor to set their hopes on the uncertainty of riches, but on God, who richly provides us with everything to enjoy. They are to do good, to be rich in good works, to be generous and ready to share, thus storing up treasure for themselves as a good foundation*

for the future, so that they may take hold of that which is truly life.
- 1 Timothy 6:17-19

In this we see the chain of God's providence. It is God who richly provides for us, and thus we are to richly provide for others as well! Doing so allows us to "take hold of that which is truly life" (eternal life, of course!). This generosity comes in two flavors: the benevolence of individual generosity and the accumulated help of the church.

And not only that, but he has been appointed by the churches to travel with us as we carry out this act of grace that is being ministered by us, for the glory of the Lord himself and to show our good will. We take this course so that no one should blame us about this generous gift that is being administered by us, for we aim at what is honorable not only in the Lord's sight but also in the sight of man.
- 2 Corinthians 8:19-21

Generosity fulfills two glorifying purposes. It elevates God directly by showing Him that His work is our priority, and it also elevates Him in the eyes of the world by demonstrating to them the riches of His grace. An essential part of glorifying God is being radically different from the world around us. Is there a better way than by forsaking the world's view of money and wealth and committing your finances to God's causes?

More money creates more options. Which option we choose demonstrates our priorities. Thus, for those who have more money than they need, what greater demonstration of priority could there be than being generous, especially in relation to the Church? This can glorify God by strengthening the body of the Lord, showing God's love to the world, or, in the case of supporting mission work, participating directly in the spread of the Gospel!

This is supposed to be cyclical, right?

> *For if the readiness is there, it is acceptable according to what a person has, not according to what he does not have. For I do not mean that others should be eased and you burdened, but that as a matter of fairness your abundance at the present time should supply their need, so that their abundance may supply your need, that there may be fairness. As it is written, "Whoever gathered much had nothing left over, and whoever gathered little had no lack."*
> - 2 Corinthians 8:12-15

The reciprocal nature of generosity is what allows it to be so glorifying to God! When I have need, God's can fulfill His providence in my life through your generosity, and when you have need, I can be God's instrument of blessing to you. In each case, God is given the glory!

But, a word of warning. Regardless of what you think about wealth inequality or societal power dynamics, more people in this country have more discretionary spending power than any other place or time in history. More people qualify as "rich" than we are perhaps comfortable admitting, according to the way the Bible talks about and defines richness.

THE BIBLICAL DEFINITION OF "RICH"

> *But godliness with contentment is great gain, for we brought nothing into the world, and we cannot take*

anything out of the world. But if we have food and clothing, with these we will be content.
  - *1 Timothy 6:6-8*

With what are we supposed to be content? Having the latest phone or the nicest car? Paul says we should be content with "food and clothing." Jesus warns, "Take care, and be on your guard against all covetousness, for one's life does not consist in the abundance of his possessions" (Luke 12:15). The key word there is "abundance" or having excess.

What did Paul quote in 2 Corinthians 8:15? "Whoever gathered much had nothing left over, and whoever gathered little had no lack." There is almost no discussion in the New Testament about relative income brackets. It seems to be the case that in the minds of the New Testament writers (and Jesus), there were only three categories: the poor (who didn't have enough), the rich (those who had more than enough), and the rest.

So, who do all the passages about the rich in the New Testament apply to? Who are they directed at? What is the magical income number where you don't have to worry about the fact that "it is easier for a camel to go through the eye of a needle than for a rich person to enter the kingdom of God" (Luke 18:25)?

Is it $60k a year? $100k? Or maybe it's based on percentage; if you make 200x the poverty line, you are rich. Of course such talk is absurd. Go back and read every scripture included in this chapter. There is only one distinction between the rich and everyone else: the rich have more than they need.

THE COMPLEX MATTER OF "NEED"

Do you have more than you need? Before we can answer

that, we have to define "need." The baseline definition in the Bible seems to be "able to survive," but there are a lot of components to mere "survival." To survive, we need the basics: food, shelter, and clothing. But to get those basics, most of us have to spend money. To get money, we have to have a job. So, could the argument be made that anything required to maintain your job is a necessity? That might include a car or a phone or a laptop, even though those objects are not strictly needed for survival. Maybe we could be more nuanced than that; perhaps you "need" a phone for your job, but do you need the most expensive one or the nicest one? What about your car? Do you need one that has all the most recent technology and luxuries?

On the other hand, we know that life is more than just survival. Jesus himself asks, "Is not life more than food, and the body more than clothing?" (Matthew 6:25). God told Israel He would abundantly bless them if they obeyed the commandments, so we know that it must not be inherently wrong to enjoy abundant pleasure in life. (Please don't think I'm espousing the prosperity Gospel; we know that God hasn't promised to Christians physical success as a reward for faithfulness. My point is that physical success cannot be inherently wrong, or else God would not have given it to Israel!)

But the general point is simple: If you have more than what you need, you should be reading the passages that talk about the rich as words directly pointed at you! The warnings are for you and the instructions are for you! Stop thinking about them as instructions "for someone else," and think about how your life reflects what these Scriptures say.

Some More Complications

> *But those who desire to be rich fall into temptation, into a snare, into many senseless and harmful desires that plunge people into ruin and destruction. For the love of money is a root of all kinds of evils. It is through this craving that some have wandered away from the faith and pierced themselves with many pangs.*
> *- 1 Timothy 6:9-10*

It is unfortunate but true that with more money comes more opportunities to dishonor God through our spending. We need to be thoughtful and considerate. What message does our spending send to the world? What priorities are we demonstrating to God? Let us consider some nuanced scenarios that might inform our view of glorifying God with money.

First, is it wrong to buy things from people who support unrighteousness? Does buying something equal an endorsement of the seller's ideals? If the answer is "only sometimes" then how can we draw the line?

While the Bible doesn't address these questions directly, we might consider a passage like Ephesians 5:

> *For you may be sure of this, that everyone who is sexually immoral or impure, or who is covetous (that is, an idolater), has no inheritance in the kingdom of Christ and God. Let no one deceive you with empty words, for because of these things the wrath of God comes upon the sons of disobedience. Therefore do not become partners with them; for at one time you were darkness, but now you are light in the Lord. Walk as children of light (for the fruit of light is found in all that is good and right and true), and try to discern what is*

pleasing to the Lord. Take no part in the unfruitful works of darkness, but instead expose them.
- Ephesians 5:5-11

What exactly is entailed by the phrases "do not become partners" and "take no part in"? Does this mean we shouldn't support them by giving them money in exchange for goods and services? For the sake of argument, let's assume for a bit that this text is telling us we should not do business with those who support unrighteousness. Let's follow this line of reasoning to the end.

"Vote with your wallet" is the central tenet of this view, right? The ultimate intent is that the business will make less money until they change their values or priorities. If they aren't willing to change their ideals, they will go out of business. This assumes that the main person who will feel the effects of your decision will be the corporate owner. What about all the local workers who may or may not agree with the corporation? If we shouldn't buy from that business, surely we must think that working for them is wrong as well! Are we willing to support the workers who lost their jobs because enough of us voted with our wallet and a local franchise went out of business?

We know good people who work for corporations who publicly support unrighteous ideas. Do we honestly expect them to quit? What if they can't find another job? Should they become "worse than an unbeliever" by refusing to provide for their families?

Where is the line? When is a corporate stance sinful enough to warrant ending your business with them? In Ephesians 5, Paul is saying not to partner with "the sexually immoral, the impure, or the covetous." That might be a very large percentage of business owners; impure is such a broad term! Very few businesses are explicitly Christian. Should we stop shopping at the 90% of stores that aren't? Are we willing to pay higher prices to do so (because the lowest prices are usually found at the megacorporations who generally do not support Christian ideals)?

Many places sell alcohol. If you think drinking or drunkenness is wrong, is it right to support a business that enables that act? Where are you going to buy gas (since most, if not all, gas stations also sell alcohol)? Most movie studios make a mix of family friendly and immoral content; should you stop seeing movies altogether because of the immoral movies a company makes?

Also, when you think a corporate stance is worthy of a boycott and your fellow Christian doesn't, who is right? How can you settle such a disagreement?

How about this: if it is wrong to support businesses that espouse unrighteous ideals, should we be shopping on Sunday? When we eat out on Sunday, we take advantage of the fact that people are not attending a local assembly of worship. If we want everyone to go to church, shouldn't we be engaging in habits that facilitate that? Many of these questions are very hard to answer and may not have absolute answers, but these are the questions we must consider once we start down the path of prescribing where we should or shouldn't spend our money.

A POSSIBLE ANSWER

As is my habit, I've taken an idea to the extreme to make a point. The Bible isn't explicit about many of these questions because they are a result of extreme societal wealth. In the first century, people didn't have a dozen options for where to buy a pair of sandals. As manufacturing costs have decreased and discretionary buying power has exploded, businesses and purchasing options have proliferated at an astonishing rate.

> *"All things are lawful," but not all things are helpful. "All things are lawful," but not all things build up. Let no one seek his own good, but the good of his neighbor. Eat whatever is sold in the meat market without raising any question on the ground of conscience. For "the earth is the Lord's, and the fullness thereof." If one of the unbelievers invites you to dinner and you are disposed to go, eat whatever is set before you without raising any question on the ground of conscience. But if someone says to you, "This has been offered in sacrifice," then do not eat it, for the sake of the one who informed you, and for the sake of conscience— I do not mean your conscience, but his. For why should my liberty be determined by someone else's conscience? If I partake with thankfulness, why am I denounced because of that for which I give thanks? So, whether you eat or drink, or whatever you do, do all to the glory of God. Give no offense to Jews or to Greeks or to the church of God, just as I try to please everyone in everything I do, not seeking my own advantage, but that of many, that they may be saved.*
> - 1 Corinthians 10:23-33

These questions are quintessential examples of what Paul grappled with in 1 Corinthians 10! Paul saw nothing explicitly wrong with eating the meat sacrificed to idols. Is supporting homosexuality (as many modern corporations do) worse than idol worship? If not, why would Paul prohibit shopping at such a corporation? Paul seems to be saying "don't worry about it" but, at the same time, he explicitly commands us to consider how our actions will affect the people in our lives.

This is a profound general principle to apply to money (and

many other matters). Yes, it's your money, but how you spend it, especially on things that are publicly known, affects more people than just you! We need to be thoughtful about how our spending reflects our priorities and values and how our decisions influence other people.

Thus, we see one possible reason why the Bible focuses so much on generosity. Being generous is the easiest way to avoid all these complex issues. By giving your money to God and helping others, you spend your money in an obviously righteous way, one that demonstrates God's place in your life and provides an opportunity to share the gospel with others.

A FINAL WARNING

We must be careful not to let money take the place of service. It can be easy to write a check on Sunday and feel satisfied about our Christian good works, but money is not a replacement for time or effort. Let us return once more to 1 Timothy:

> *As for the rich in this present age, charge them not to be haughty, nor to set their hopes on the uncertainty of riches, but on God, who richly provides us with everything to enjoy. They are to do good, to be rich in good works, to be generous and ready to share, thus storing up treasure for themselves as a good foundation for the future, so that they may take hold of that which is truly life.*
>
> *- 1 Timothy 6:17-19*

"Doing good," "being rich in good works," and "being generous" are separate things. Money can't be a replacement for good works! Money is a supplement and complement to good works, and being generous could be one of the good works we do, but if we are to be "rich" in good works, then we need to have an abundance of them, right? If the Bible uses the word "rich" to mean "having more than you need," then we should be seeking the most possible good works, not the bare minimum! We should be doing more good works than may be strictly necessary, looking for every opportunity to serve God and others.

Finally, remember that purchasing decisions are a function of our priorities. We all make choices. Maybe you need a phone for work, but do you need the latest iPhone every six months? You probably need a car to get to work, but does it have to be the latest and greatest Mercedes? The Bible doesn't say it's wrong to have nice things, but the Bible warns us time and time again not to let money, riches, and wealth get in the way of serving God. If we want to glorify God, we need to put Him first. Putting God first in our financial habits requires thoughtfulness, purpose, and wisdom. May we all have wisdom as we consider how we spend our money in the way that most glorifies God!

Digging Deeper

1. Do you consider yourself to be rich, poor, or somewhere in the middle? If people of Jesus's day could experience your life, how do you think they would define your status?

2. Take some time this week to categorize your spending. What percentage of your money goes to necessities, luxuries, spiritual things, etc.? If you don't know how to do this, is there someone who could help you?

3. What planning process do you use to determine your spending (do you even plan at all)? At what stage in your planning do you decide how much to give to God?

4. Is there anyone you know that you could be a financial blessing to? How could you help them? What keeps you from doing so?

12. Broken Glory: Glorifying God when it Hurts

My father-in-law died in 2019. He was my wife's other best friend. They called each other every day. He had a heart attack and then was gone five days later, never waking back up. They didn't get to say goodbye.

It's the kind of thing that can break someone.

She has told me multiple times that her relationship with God has only grown stronger since his passing. It is amazing to me. She has grown stronger spiritually, even though she has been shattered and broken emotionally and intellectually. Even though she is heartbroken and doesn't understand, she has continued to exalt God throughout. I'm sure most of you can bring to mind someone in a similar circumstance or have experienced this grief yourself. Maybe it wasn't the death of a loved one; maybe it was cancer or some other kind of life crisis like losing a job or a home or a natural disaster. Through it all, you or they keep giving God the glory.

How? This is the question I keep asking myself.

Scripture is full of men and women who exalted God in the depths of despair; who, in the midst of horror and sorrow, continued to elevate Him. Some of them even thought God must be to blame for their struggles, but they still honored, praised, and exalted Him, both publicly and privately. How did they do this?

DAVID'S SIN

Let's first return to a story we have previously examined. David, after his sin with Bathsheba, was told that his punishment would be horrible; the child conceived by David's sinful act would not live. For a time, David lamented, wept, and fasted, actions we would expect of a grieving person. He said it was because he was trying to convince God to relent (2 Samuel 12:22). We can understand, right? Have you ever wanted something so desperately that your pursuit of God's providence consumed your whole life?

Nevertheless, we know that God did not relent. The child died. *I would have been so angry!* This is not like a child dying today of some ailment or accident. Sometimes horrible things happen in a fallen world (Romans 8:20-22), and it's not anyone's fault. Sometimes horrible things happen because people are selfish and make bad choices. I think we all understand that. But this was caused by God! I cannot imagine the swirl of emotions and bitterness most (including myself) would feel. But what did David do?

> *But when David saw that his servants were whispering together, David understood that the child was dead. And David said to his servants, "Is the child dead?" They said, "He is dead." Then David arose from the earth and washed and anointed himself and changed his clothes. And he went into the house of the Lord and worshiped. He then went to his own house. And when he asked, they set food before him, and he ate.*
> *- 2 Samuel 12:19-20*

What was the *first thing* he did when he learned of his child's death (a death very much caused by the Lord)? *He went into the house of the Lord and worshipped.* Can you even fathom this? Can we conceive of the kind of dedication and heart required to respond to the death of a child with *worship*?!

Sorrow and grief, even the kind that are caused by the death of a child, are not valid excuses to stop glorifying God. This attitude must be a major part of the reason why David was called "a man after God's own heart" (Acts 13:22). David sought God's will in all things, even at the expense of his own desires (1 Samuel 24:6, for example).

This might seem above and beyond what should be expected of a person. Yet David glorified God, even as he was broken inside.

Is this honestly what God expects of His children? Let's consider the suffering of another man…

Job's Suffering

Job, like David, was a man well acquainted with sorrow, yet Job seemed to respond more with anger and bitterness than David did.

If you don't remember the story of Job, go read the first three chapters. The Devil went to God, and God essentially bragged about how great Job was. The Devil accused God of protecting Job, and God allowed Satan to eventually take Job's health, family, and possessions. This ends, predictably, with Job sitting around a fire, depressed and destitute, angry and bitter.

To me, one of the saddest parts of the story is that it seems like Job never got to know *why*. All he knew was that he was suffering under such a weight of sorrow and that he couldn't see any reason why he should be. The debate between him and his friends, that takes up most of the book, centers on whether or not Job's suffering is his own fault. Was God punishing him for wickedness? This is how Job felt:

> *Though I am in the right, I cannot answer him;*
> *I must appeal for mercy to my accuser.*
>   *If I summoned him and he answered me,*
> *I would not believe that he was listening to my voice.*
>   *For he crushes me with a tempest*
> *and multiplies my wounds without cause;*
>   *he will not let me get my breath,*
> *but fills me with bitterness.*
> - Job 9:15-18

> *"Today also my complaint is bitter;*
> *my hand is heavy on account of my groaning.*
> - Job 23:2

Have you ever felt this way; felt deep in your bones that your suffering was unjust, undeserved? Felt bitterness and anger that you could not argue with God face to face? I know I have. It is a very natural response to the suffering of the righteous. Job knew that feeling!

Yet, Job kept elevating and glorifying God!

> *Though he slay me, I will hope in him;*
> *yet I will argue my ways to his face.*
>   *This will be my salvation,*
> *that the godless shall not*
> *come before him.*
> - Job 13:15-16

> *"From where, then, does wisdom come?*
> *And where is the place of understanding?*

It is hidden from the eyes of all living
and concealed from the birds of the air.
  Abaddon and Death say,
  'We have heard a rumor of it with our ears.'
"God understands the way to it,
and he knows its place.
  For he looks to the ends of the earth
  and sees everything under the heavens.
- Job 28:20-24

Job was struggling with a cognitive dissonance (trying to reconcile two seemingly contradictory ideas). He knew that God was infinitely wise, almighty, and pure, yet he also knew that he had done nothing wrong. Job was righteous! Job's view of God held that God was responsible for all things (it is unclear whether Job even knew about the Devil). So, Job's mind was confused. How could God be wise and pure and responsible for all things and yet righteous Job be suffering so much? How could a just God allow this to happen or even cause it to happen?!

This dissonance caused him anger and bitterness, as I think it does for many people today. It is easy to want to apply our sense of justice to the struggles we see all around us. If a person is righteous, they should prosper! However, we know that this isn't the case, and when calamity comes upon us it's easy to slip into anger and bitterness.

Yet we know that Job held on to God's glory:

In all this Job did not sin or charge God with wrong.
- Job 1:22

Despite Job's anger and bitterness, he continued to glorify God. His anger did not prevent him from placing God on the highest place. Even as he was accusing God, he did so with the understanding that there must be an explanation that he simply couldn't understand. It's not wrong to feel angry and bitter if we continually acknowledge that our anger and bitterness comes from our own limited understanding. In fact, we *should* bring our anger and bitterness to God (1 Peter 5:7). If we keep admitting that God knows what He's doing, if we can stop ourselves from accusing God of wrongdoing, we can continue to exalt God even though we are angry at Him! In some ways it's like a conflict in a marriage; every marriage has disagreements, but such things only lead to divorce when people stop giving each other the benefit of the doubt. Give God the benefit of the doubt (especially since we know that God is perfectly just, unlike all spouses). We know how it ended for Job:

> *After the Lord had spoken these words to Job, the Lord said to Eliphaz the Temanite: "My anger burns against you and against your two friends, for you have not spoken of me what is right, as my servant Job has.*
> *- Job 42:7*

In the end, Job must have maintained a pure attitude toward God because God says that Job "spoke right" of Him. God did eventually confront Job when it seemed like Job might go too far, but when He did, Job immediately backed down and exalted God, despite Job's personal feelings about what had happened.

PAUL'S THORN

Finally, we return to Paul and his "thorn in the flesh" (which we examined in the second chapter). No one knows what Paul's thorn in the flesh was; perhaps it was a speech impediment or a bodily infirmity or even an evil spirit or a bitter rival. All we know is that Paul hated it:

> *So to keep me from becoming conceited because of the surpassing greatness of the revelations, a thorn was given me in the flesh, a messenger of Satan to harass me, to keep me from becoming conceited. Three times I pleaded with the Lord about this, that it should leave me.*
> - 2 Corinthians 12:7-8

He *pleaded* to the Lord. Have you ever pleaded with God? Maybe you want God to alleviate some suffering or change some life circumstance or remove some horrible person from your life. We all understand what it's like to have a thorn in the flesh. David's primary emotions were guilt and sadness, Job's were anger and bitterness, but Paul's primary emotions seemed to be desperation and frustration.

How did the Lord reply?

> *But he said to me, "My grace is sufficient for you, for my power is made perfect in weakness."*
> - 2 Corinthians 12:9

The Lord told Paul "no."

Remember this: *Sometimes God tells us no*! When He does, it can surely be awful! God told David, "No, you cannot have your child." God told Job, "No, you cannot have the answers you seek or the people you lost." God told Paul "No, you cannot have relief from your suffering." God told all these people no! Yet, what did Paul do next?

> *Therefore I will boast all the more gladly of my weaknesses, so that the power of Christ may rest upon me. For the sake of Christ, then, I am content with*

weaknesses, insults, hardships, persecutions, and calamities. For when I am weak, then I am strong.
- 2 Corinthians 12:9-10

Isn't this the epitome of glorifying God? To let God's power in your life take precedence, to allow His greatness to be your strength and highest priority? To allow His will to rule your life, even when you are being torn apart by tragic circumstance or emotion?

Paul was content in whatever suffering he faced because that same suffering gave him the opportunity to put Christ in a higher position in his life. It made him lean on the Lord more! It allowed him to more fully demonstrate the power of God to the people around him!

We don't know what this thorn in the flesh was, but Paul (inspired by the Spirit) intentionally withheld that information. It doesn't matter what your thorn in the flesh is! Our weakness does not detract from God's glory. It provides an avenue for it to increase, but only if we can let go of our frustration and submit to God's answer, even if that answer seems to be no. Paul told the Corinthians in the same letter:

> *But we have this treasure in jars of clay, to show that the surpassing power belongs to God and not to us. We are afflicted in every way, but not crushed; perplexed, but not driven to despair; persecuted, but not forsaken; struck down, but not destroyed; always carrying in the body the death of Jesus, so that the life of Jesus may also be manifested in our bodies. For we who live are always being given over to death for Jesus' sake, so that the life of Jesus also may be manifested in our mortal flesh.*
> - 2 Corinthians 4:7-11

We are but mere jars, containing something truly wonderful, a treasure beyond measure. We manifest the life of Jesus, and wasn't his life full of righteous suffering? Even if we are given over to death, we can still show the world the treasure of God's glory!

BALANCING GLORY AND EMOTION

David, Job, and Paul felt deeply. They felt horribly. Their hearts ran the gamut from sorrow to bitterness, anger to desperation. Yet they still put God in the highest place and endeavored to understand His will for their lives; when God told them "no," they submitted.

I don't know what you are going through, but I am confident that there is something in your life that is a cause of pain. It isn't sinful to feel what you feel! The world we live in is full of sorrow and pain and horror. God created us with these emotions; emotions that He himself feels (Genesis 6:5-7; Deuteronomy 9:16-21). These emotions are good and powerful motivators for action and compassion for others. Feeling sadness or anger only diminishes God when we allow those feelings to control us and cause us to act contrary to God's will. We feel what we feel, but those feelings do not give us license to disregard the glory of God.

Feeling such raw, powerful emotions and still choosing to trust in God and exalt Him is *immensely* glorifying. It's easy to like God when times are good, but if we can still put God first and proclaim His glory when it seems like He is allowing us to suffer, that is true faith and exaltation. Remember that faithful acknowledgment of God and His position, righteousness, and authority is the first step to glorifying God. It's why the Hebrew writer includes so many examples in the "hall of faith":

> *Women received back their dead by resurrection. Some were tortured, refusing to accept release, so that they might rise again to a better life. Others suffered mocking and flogging, and even chains and imprisonment. They were stoned, they were sawn in two, they were killed with the sword. They went about in skins of sheep and goats, destitute, afflicted, mistreated— of whom the world was not worthy— wandering about in deserts and mountains, and in dens and caves of the earth.*
>
> *- Hebrews 11:35-38*

Of whom the world was not worthy. This may be my favorite line in the entire Bible. Remaining faithful and exalting God, even in the midst of affliction, is the thing that should separate the Christian from the world. Peter told us that, far from being a cause for despair, righteous suffering should be a cause of joy (1 Peter 4:12-14)!

This powerful kind of faithfulness is what enables us to stand apart from the mundane concerns of politics, even when those politics result in our suffering. It is what empowers us to sacrifice our money or our desires to serve God; if I can glorify God when my parent or child dies, then how hard can it be to glorify God by spending less money on selfish things or controlling my sexual impulses? It is what unifies us as part of God's glorious temple; we all know what it's like to suffer, so we all know what really matters in this life and the next!

If we allow *God* to shape our pain and brokenness, instead of allowing *them* to use and shape us, these things can help us have a closer relationship with God. If we are open and honest with those around us, as these three men were about their brokenness, our enduring faithfulness can be an incredibly powerful agent of God's glory among the lost.

Digging Deeper

1. Are there things God has done (either in the Bible or in your own life) that cause you to doubt or question? What have you done to address that doubt?

2. Have you ever known anyone who remained steadfastly faithful even in dreadful circumstances? How did they affect you? How can you emulate them?

3. What are some ways we can glorify God even when we don't feel like it, or when we feel sad or depressed?

4. Is there anyone in your life who is broken right now? How can you bring glory to God by helping and encouraging them? List some tangible things you could do to support them (and then do them!).

13. Glory in Freedom: When our Purpose is Confusing

How many decisions does the average person make every day? A brief internet search yields a wide range of numbers, from 70 to 35,000; 35,000 seems absurd to me, but surely, it's at least dozens or even hundreds. We decide what to wear, what to eat, how to eat, what to say; and these are just the normal, everyday things!

Most of these decisions contain almost no inherent morality. God has not prescribed what you should have for lunch on a given Thursday nor at what time of day you should get out of bed. Yes, we know that even these things might be governed by general principles or commands, but the minutia, the logistics, are, for the most part, left up to us to decide.

It is in this incredible moral freedom that we find an interesting component of glorifying God. When so many of the details of our lives are left up to us, how do we most effectively glorify God? We know that obeying His commands glorifies Him, so how should we glorify Him beyond obedience to explicit commands? If we are to glorify God "in whatever [we] do," then what about decisions like where to live, what job to pursue, or how many kids to have? These are big, important parts of our life, but God has given us the liberty to choose.

However, even though God hasn't prescribed specific aspects of these important subjects, certain choices still might glorify God more than others! Therein lies the difficulty: If I am to truly glorify God in all that I do, then surely these decisions matter, even if God hasn't imposed moral restrictions upon their details.

ALL THINGS ARE LAWFUL

In this concluding chapter I want to reinforce some ideas we have previously discussed. Let's return to the core text of this study:

> *"All things are lawful," but not all things are helpful. "All things are lawful," but not all things build up. Let no one seek his own good, but the good of his neighbor. Eat whatever is sold in the meat market without raising any question on the ground of conscience. For "the earth is the Lord's, and the fullness thereof." If one of the unbelievers invites you to dinner and you are disposed to go, eat whatever is set before you without raising any question on the ground of conscience. But if someone says to you, "This has been offered in sacrifice," then do not eat it, for the sake of the one who informed you, and for the sake of conscience— I do not mean your conscience, but his. For why should my liberty be determined by someone else's conscience? If I partake with thankfulness, why am I denounced because of that for which I give thanks?*
>
> *So, whether you eat or drink, or whatever you do, do all to the glory of God. Give no offense to Jews or to Greeks or to the church of God, just as I try to please*

everyone in everything I do, not seeking my own advantage, but that of many, that they may be saved.
- 1 Corinthians 10:23-33

We have expounded upon various elements of this text throughout this book, and we won't rehash most of it. But this is actually the second time in 1 Corinthians that Paul uses the phrase "all things are lawful." The first is a few chapters prior:

"All things are lawful for me," but not all things are helpful. "All things are lawful for me," but I will not be dominated by anything. "Food is meant for the stomach and the stomach for food"—and God will destroy both one and the other. The body is not meant for sexual immorality, but for the Lord, and the Lord for the body. And God raised the Lord and will also raise us up by his power. Do you not know that your bodies are members of Christ? Shall I then take the members of Christ and make them members of a prostitute? Never!
- 1 Corinthians 6:12-15

This text occurs in the midst of a discussion of sexual sin and righteousness, and we will return to that topic in a moment. Note first what he follows up with: "I will not be dominated by anything." This is the first principle of these free choices, these decisions that God has left up to us. Yes, outside of some overall commands, God hasn't prescribed where you should live or what job you should have or what your hobbies should be. But anything that dominates your life, or controls you instead of you controlling it, becomes an obstacle for glorifying God! When something matters more in our decision-making than God's potential glory, then we have become dominated by that thing!

A Case Study: Sex and Marriage

This section of the text concludes with a verse that is very relevant for our discussion:

> *Or do you not know that your body is a temple of the Holy Spirit within you, whom you have from God? You are not your own, for you were bought with a price. So glorify God in your body*
> *- 1 Corinthians 6:19-20*

Certainly, the main point in 1 Corinthians 6-7 concerns sexual purity, but how many things do we do with our bodies? Where we go, how we act, what we say; these can all be matters of the flesh if we are controlled by something other than a desire to glorify God!

Continuing in the text, we see a classic example of the kind of decision we are talking about. The decision to marry is an inherently amoral one. What do I mean by that? There is no universal command to marry or remain unmarried. There are of course commands about who can marry, and under what circumstances marriage is righteous or unrighteous, and even some commands about who you should marry; but the decision to get married is not commanded one way or another. A person can live a fully righteous, purposeful life without getting married, just like a person can live a selfish, horrible life if they are married. Thus, God has given each person the *moral liberty* to get married. The decision to be married or not does not carry any moral imperative, *if* we follow all the other connected commands that God has given us that might affect this decision. You can remain unmarried and be righteous, or marry and be righteous, etc., but that doesn't mean that the decision doesn't matter:

> *Now as a concession, not a command, I say this. I wish that all were as I myself am. But each has his own gift from God, one of one kind and one of another. To the unmarried and the widows I say that it is good for them to remain single as I am. But if they cannot exercise self-control, they should marry. For it is better to marry than to burn with passion.*
> *- 1 Corinthians 7:6-9*

In Paul's mind, the choice to marry is a matter of righteousness, even though both options (to marry or not) are morally valid. He considered it "better" to remain unmarried, why?

> *I want you to be free from anxieties. The unmarried man is anxious about the things of the Lord, how to please the Lord. But the married man is anxious about worldly things, how to please his wife, and his interests are divided. And the unmarried or betrothed woman is anxious about the things of the Lord, how to be holy in body and spirit. But the married woman is anxious about worldly things, how to please her husband. I say this for your own benefit, not to lay any restraint upon you, but to promote good order and to secure your undivided devotion to the Lord.*
> *- 1 Corinthians 7:32-35*

Fair or unfair, the unmarried have, at the very least, more opportunities and time to directly devote themselves to God's glory. Being a faithful spouse and having children can indeed glorify God, but Paul seems to be saying that the efforts of the married will be divided between God's glory and the needs of the family. The person who is unmarried has more opportunity to directly pursue God's glory and elevate Him.

Paul himself embodied this marital status by the total freedom he had to pursue evangelism all over the globe, untethered to the bonds of physical family.

The point of this example, for our purposes, is this: Even decisions that seemingly carry no moral imperative often carry important ramifications for our ability to glorify God. While it isn't sinful to get married, it is undeniable that the marriage relationship splits a person's focus between God and the spouse.

So, even when I think I am making a meaningless choice, I might be choosing something that diminishes God or detracts from my ability to glorify Him in the future. We must be thoughtful about the implications and consequences of our decisions!

It's not just a matter of *what* we do but *why* we do it and what circumstances those choices might lead to that will require more choices. No choice we make exists in a vacuum; our choices form a chain that brings us closer to or takes us further from God. It may not be sinful to move to any particular town, but what if the place you are moving to has no congregation of believers? Are you prepared to do the work necessary to start one, or are you resigning yourself to not having anywhere to worship, or are you willing to drive however far you need to in order to fellowship with other Christians? Your job might not involve doing explicitly sinful things, but if it requires you to consistently work on Sunday, are you able to spiritually bear that burden?

THE DANGER OF DECISION PARALYSIS

Humans tend to overreact to things, don't we? Even recent religious history is rife with this. Various religious groups have swung back and forth along the faith-works axis, one group essentially buying salvation and the other overreacting by saying that works are totally irrelevant. Here, we see another potential problem.

It is incorrect to say that if God hasn't addressed a subject specifically, we are totally free to do whatever we want. God has at the very least indirectly addressed almost every meaningful activity of life. The Bible doesn't say anything about movies because movies weren't invented when it was written, but the Bible says many things about what we allow into our hearts and minds and the kinds of things we consume. Thus, we should thoughtfully consider what movies we choose to watch and how they might satisfy or reject the principles of Scripture.

However, we can't be so afraid of messing up that we choose to do nothing. My movie choices need to be thoughtfully considered, but that doesn't mean I need to give up on movies altogether! That's a cop out. Just because I might mess up, doesn't mean I should give up on the deciding process altogether.

> *And to the angel of the church in Laodicea write: "The words of the Amen, the faithful and true witness, the beginning of God's creation.*
> *I know your works: you are neither cold nor hot. Would that you were either cold or hot! So, because you are lukewarm, and neither hot nor cold, I will spit you out of my mouth. For you say, I am rich, I have prospered, and I need nothing, not realizing that you are wretched, pitiable, poor, blind, and naked."*
> *- Revelation 3:14-17*

This text speaks to the 21st century American Christian almost directly! Most of us are rich and have prospered and don't really need anything. So what does Jesus mean when he says they are *lukewarm*? The settlement north of Laodicea contained hot springs and the settlement south contained a source of cold water. Both of these waters had different purposes, but the city of Laodicea continually struggled with a problem; by the time the water arrived through aqueduct, it was lukewarm from either direction, not good for any use!

The Christians in Laodicea were complacent, a condition brought on by their wealth. Jesus used an example they would have been familiar with to make a simple point: be useful, do something, and don't just sit back and relax!

Some of the hardest choices in life are often not between righteousness and wickedness, but between two things that could potentially glorify God. We need to choose something! We can't just sit back and do nothing. That certainly won't result in God's glory.

So, every decision matters (at least a little bit), and we can't just sit out the decision making. This is the very essence of the Christian life! When Paul says to do "all for the glory of God," isn't this what he means? Every day we are presented with hundreds of choices. Some of those choices are made "for us" by the decision to obey God's explicit commands, but many more of them are not. We must decide which option is going to result in God's glory. How can we possibly figure out which choices to make?

> *I appeal to you therefore, brothers, by the mercies of God, to present your bodies as a living sacrifice, holy and acceptable to God, which is your spiritual worship. Do not be conformed to this world, but be transformed by the renewal of your mind, that by testing you may discern what is the will of God, what is good and acceptable and perfect.*
>
> *- Romans 12:1-2*

This passage, which we discussed in the fourth chapter, is one of the most notoriously difficult to translate and has some of the most variation between major translations. However, at the core of each translation is the same idea: The renewal of our mind leads to the discernment of that which is acceptable to God. By putting God's ideals first in our hearts, we can begin to test everything we encounter against those ideals and then begin to form a list of things that are "good and acceptable and perfect". This process applies to the jobs we pick, the places we live, the friends we make, and even to the most mundane choices of everyday life. We know that this is a long-term project:

> *For though by this time you ought to be teachers, you need someone to teach you again the basic principles of the oracles of God. You need milk, not solid food, for everyone who lives on milk is unskilled in the word of righteousness, since he is a child. But solid food is for the mature, for those who have their powers of discernment trained by constant practice to distinguish good from evil.*
>
> *- Hebrews 5:12-14*

There is a reason that Christianity is a group effort: Everyone is at different stages of this journey toward having "powers of discernment," and we only get there by "constant practice." Those who have trained for a long time should then begin to impart some of their wisdom to others (the "ought to be teachers" part of the text). The development of discernment is a collective effort, aided by the advice and instruction of others!

The need to "distinguish good from evil" applies even to the areas of liberty God has given us, where the details may not matter but God's glory still does. How often do we consider if the choices we make are elevating or exalting God, especially in those areas of "liberty"?

SOME FINAL QUESTIONS

I ended chapter six with some catchy acronyms, mental devices to help us discern the most glorifying option out of many choices. I won't repeat those here, but if you want to refresh yourself, you should do so. Instead, I want to end with some questions we should be asking ourselves when we make seemingly moral-neutral decisions. These questions might help illuminate the absolute moral right in a given circumstance and the potential problems or detriments to God's glory that might result from a seemingly innocuous choice.

1. Does this choice violate or fulfill any of God's explicit commands? It's almost too obvious, but in case we forgot, obedience is one of the primary ways we glorify God.

2. Does this choice tempt me to violate any of God's explicit commands? Many decisions aren't explicitly unrighteous but could very easily lead to behaviors that are. Consider if this decision would "lead you into temptation" (Matthew 6:13) in some way.

3. Is this choice going to leave me with more or less time to devote to God and His family? Often Christians fall away, not through a conscious decision to stop following God, but because they just got too busy. There are many good things we can do in life, and none of them are worth more than spending time serving and learning about the Creator or growing within the body of Christ.

4. Does this choice increase or decrease my opportunities to evangelize? Not only might a decision remove your ability to evangelize, but it might decrease your effectiveness when you do evangelize.

5. How could this choice be misconstrued by a combative non-Christian? Many things are amoral, but nonetheless could be used as ammunition against us by those who want to dishonor God. We have to ask ourselves if the benefit of something is worth the potential decrease to our or God's or the Church's reputation. Sometimes it is, and sometimes it isn't.

6. Does this choice offend the conscience of one of my fellow Christians? This is very closely related to number 1, since being considerate of our weaker family members is in fact an explicit command.

7. Does this choice encourage others to glorify God or dishonor Him? Our actions do not just affect us! Part of being "the light of the world" is acting in such a way that others want to exalt the God we serve.

CONCLUSION

Ultimately, glorifying God requires purpose, commitment, knowledge, and intentionality. Jesus demonstrated these qualities over and over again, and so did His apostles, even though they occasionally messed up. If this book has done nothing else, I pray that it has stirred up thought in your heart about how best we can glorify God together.

To God be the glory!

Digging Deeper

1. What are some areas of life in which God has not commanded anything of us one way or another? What are some things that God has commanded us to do, but has remained silent about how we should do them?

2. How should we respond when fellow Christians choose differently than us in these areas of life? How do you want your fellow Christians to respond to your choices in these matters?

3. Do you think you have a highly developed skill of discernment? If not, what can you do to improve? Is there anyone you could ask for help?

4. List some tangible ways you could change your life tomorrow to glorify God more with your life. What prevents you from implementing these changes?

SCRIPTURE INDEX

Genesis
1:26-27 .... 2, 86
2:23-25 86
2:24-25 79
6:5-7 154

Leviticus
10:1-3 26
18:22 86

Deuteronomy
9:16-21 154

1 Samuel
13 18
13:10-14 19
15:7-9 21
15:14-15 21
15:24 21
17 22
24:6 148

2 Samuel
7:2 23
7:4-7 23
7:10-16 23
7:27-28 24
11-12 24
12:13 24
12:13-14 25
12:19-20 147
12:20 25
12:22 147

1 Kings
5-9 40
5:2-5 40
6:11-13 41
8:10-11 41
8:27-30 45

Esther
1:4 11

Job
1:22 150
9:15-18 149
13:15-16 149
23:2 149
28:20-24 150
42:7 151

Pslams
51:14-17 25

Ecclesiastes
7:10 113

Isaiah
43:5-7 3

Jeremiah
17:9 90

Ezekiel
16 11
43:5 10

Malachi
2:13-16 86

Matthew
4 29
4:8 11
5:13-16 60
5:14 46
5:14-16 .... 4, 120
5:16 46
5:27-29 36
5:29-30 124
6 30
6:1-18 17
6:4, 6, 18 31
6:13 166
6:21-23 119
6:25 138

7:12	127
7:13-14	112
12:36-37	124
12:46-50	72
14:23	29
15:16-19	30
16:24-25	92
19:1-9	86
22:15-22	67
23	30
25:34, 41	2

Mark

6:45-47	29
16:15	117

Luke

9:29	53
12:15	137
14:10	11
17:20-21	99
18:25	137
19:10	6
20:22-26	105

John

3:20-21	121
3:25-30	7
3:29-30	17
5:37	53
13:34-35	46
16:2	33
17:14-18	59
17:20-22	46
18:33-37	100

Acts

6:1-7	70
10	70
11:19	70
13:22	148

17	117
17:24	44
22:11	11

Romans

1:26-27	80, 87, 90
2:14-16	88, 90
2:21-24	7
2:23-24	124
6:1-6	34
8:20-22	147
8:5-8	36
8:31-39	29
9:1-2	61
9:22-23	4
12:1-2	32, 164
12:2	37
12:14-21	58
13:1-2	68
13:1-7	67
13:12-14	89, 90
14:14-20	55
15:1-7	49

1 Corinthians

1:11-13	43
2:12-14	73
3:3-4	43
3:16-17	42
5:9-10	60
6:4-7	128
6:9-10	87
6:12-15	159
6:18-20	31
6:19-20	160
7:6-9	161
7:32-35	161
8:4-6	55
9:22	117

9:24-26 126
10:23-30 55
10:23-33 .... 142, 159
10:31 .... 3, 117
10:31-33 56
10:32 57
11:2-16 86
11:13-16 .... 88, 90
11:26 6
14:33-37 86
15:50 100

2 Corinthians
4:3-4 83
4:7-11 153
5 71
5:7 53
5:16-19 71
8:12-15 136
8:15 137
8:19-21 135
10-12 12
10:13 12
10:17-18 12
11:30 12
12:7-8 152
12:7-10 .... 13, 93
12:9 152
12:9-10 153

Galatians
2:11-13 122
3:28-29 70
5:16-17 90

Ephesians
4:29 123
5:5-11 140
5:11-16 122

Philippians
1:9-11 37
1:27 47
2:1-3 48
3 71
3:17-19 37
3:18-19 85
3:18-21 66
3:19 68
4:5 106
4:8 .... 119, 127
4:8-9 38

Colossians
3:1-10 35
4:5-6 .... 62, 81, 123

1 Thessalonians
5:19-22 52

2 Thessalonians
3:10-12 133

1 Timothy
1:8-11 87
2:1-2 109
2:1-4 67
2:2 67
2:3-4 109
2:8-15 86
3:15 115
5:7-8 133
6:6-8 137
6:6-9 131
6:9-10 139
6:17-19 .... 135, 143

2 Timothy
2:3-4 67
2:24-26 91

Titus
3:1-2 105

3:1-11 67
3:8-9 107

Hebrews
3:3-6 44
5:12-14 165
5:13-14 62
6:4-8 29
9:1 33
9:6 33
11:13-16 103
11:25 121
11:35-38 155
13:4 79

James
1:5 128
1:5-6 62
3:8-14 125

1 Peter
2:9 109
2:11 66
2:11-12 ....5, 53, 102
2:12 ....55, 110
2:13-17 ....54, 104
3:1-7 86
4:1 57
4:1-5 57
4:8-11 50
4:12-14 ....112, 155
4:13-16 61
5:7 151

2 Peter
2:20-22 29
3:16 68

Revelation
3:14-17 163
13 68

Made in the USA
Coppell, TX
01 September 2022